A Victorian Diary of Newick, Sussex

1875 – 1899

Tony Turk

First published 1999 by Tony Turk,
42, Church Lane,
Mill End,
Rickmansworth,
Hertfordshire, WD3 2HD

ISBN 0 9536967 0 7

Designed and produced by
Axxent Ltd,
The Short Run Book Company,
St Stephen's House, Arthur Road,
Windsor, Berkshire SL4 1RY

The book is available from the author A R TURK, 42, Church Lane, Mill End, Rickmansworth, Hertfordshire, WD3 2HD (telephone 01923 720168) at the cover price plus postage and packing and from the following organisations and clubs in the village:

Newick Bonfire Society

Newick Cricket Club

Newick Football Club

Newick Old Pupils

The First Newick Scout Group

It is also available at the general stores (SVS Stores) on The Green, Newick News and General Store in Newick Drive, at The Post Office in Allington Road and from other selected shops.

Proceeds from the sales will be for the above clubs and societies and for the Newick Distress Trust charity.

CONTENTS

LIST OF ILLUSTRATIONS

ACKNOWLEDGEMENTS

The British Library Newspaper Library has been most helpful with the wealth of Victorian newspapers available. The staff at The Public Record Office at Kew and at The East Sussex Record Office at Lewes have been most courteous and helpful in supplying information. Access to the Sussex Archaeological Society library has been very useful. Libraries in Lewes, Brighton, Worthing, Burgess Hill etc have provided information.

Newick residents, past residents and others have assisted in supplying information and photographs, including D Wickens, J Wood, J Thomas, R Bird, J Potten and others.

Special thanks are due to John R Sclater who has not only supplied some fine photographs but has also given valuable assistance in helping to finance the book. The Sclater family has for many years, including in the Victorian times, contributed greatly to the village and this is John's contribution to marking the birth of a new millennium in Newick.

INTRODUCTION

The last 25 years of the nineteenth century was a most exciting and eventful period in Newick's history. The present school had recently opened, the railway arrived, the church was enlarged, football and cricket clubs formed, a new Reading Room built, the Parish Council created, the village pump on The Green built to commemorate Queen Victoria's Jubilee, the Horticultural Society re-formed, decent drainage provided together with balls, dances, parades, concerts, Guy Fawkes celebrations, other social activities and much more.

This was the time of Queen Victoria's dominating world-wide British Empire. Benjamin Disraeli and William Gladstone were two of the prime ministers of that time. British soldiers were engaged in battles in Africa. Gas lighting was in use in towns and cities but electricity was in its early development. Telegraph communication was operating. Telephones were in their infancy. Wireless was just invented. Travelling was by foot, railway and horse and carriage with cycling rapidly becoming more popular. Cars were only just coming on the scene. The building of a Channel Tunnel was being discussed. Photography was developing fast. And the little village of Newick in the Sussex countryside was happily getting on with life.

It has been said that the only true history of a country is to be found in its newspapers. The details for this diary have been mainly found in the local newspapers of the time – The East Sussex Journal, The East Sussex News, The Sussex Advertiser, The Sussex Agricultural Express (later known as The Sussex Express), The Sussex Daily News, The Mid Sussex Times, The Southern Weekly News, the very short lived Central Sussex Free Press and the curiously titled County Chronicle and Mark Lane Journal. These newspapers are available for inspection at The British Library Newspaper Library in Colindale, North London. Some are also available at The East Sussex Record Office in Lewes, Brighton Reference Library, Worthing library etc. Other sources of information are listed at the end of the book.

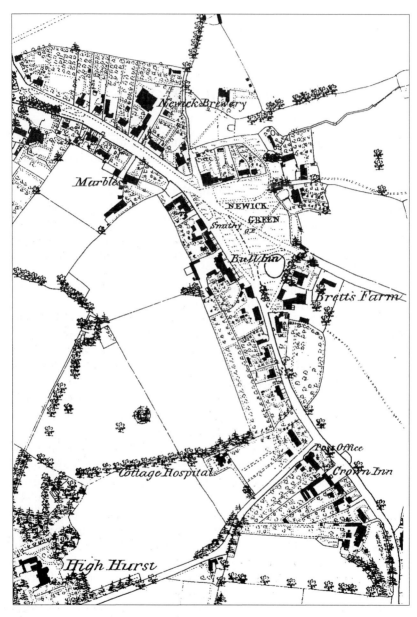

Newick Green 1873

JANUARY 1875

The annual Tradesmans Club dinner was held at The Crown Inn, courtesy of Mrs Helen Keeling. A two hour extension of time was kindly granted by Petty Sessions.

FEBRUARY 1875

The annual hunting festival was held – the Cuckfield Harriers chased their first hare from Mr Brook's land to Netherhall, Fletching Mill, William Martin's estate, Birchland, and to Rotherfield Farm. The next hare was drawn on Mr Sclater's land and chased on to Broomlye and Sharps etc. The party returned to the Bull Inn for a fine supper with the appropriate toasts and singing.

Richard Gravely, the Newick surgeon and Medical Officer of Health for the area, has prepared his annual report to the Chailey Union Rural Sanitary Authority. He comments on the miserable state of the dwellings, within the Union, in which the poorer classes live, engendering a want of personal respect.

MARCH 1875

The Education Department at Whitehall is now requiring the Parish to have a School Board under the 1875 Education Act. Members have been elected.

APRIL 1875

R Fuller and D Watson have been appointed as Overseers for Newick. The Surveyor will be J Howell.

MAY 1875

The Rev William Powell from Newick spoke at the meeting at the Maidens Head Hotel in Uckfield concerning the need for better railway connections for passengers at Tunbridge Wells. At the same time, he spoke, somewhat cynically, about the now abandoned works of the railway line which was to have run from Uckfield, past Newick, to Balcombe.

Correspondence in the newspaper objects to the netting of fish in the River Ouse at the expense of rod and line fishermen.

JUNE 1875

James Perkins, the butler for J H Sclater at Newick Park, was accidentally drowned while bathing in a pond at the Park.

The first meeting of the School Board for the Parish was held at Newick Park with J H Sclater (chairman), John Howell (vice-chairman), Thomas Roswell, Mr Blencowe and Mr Weston. The clerk is William Funnell.

JULY 1875

The industrial school at Chailey, in the old workhouse, is now opened taking in those youngsters found begging, those found destitute being orphans that have frequented the company of reputed thieves and those with no settled place or proper guardianship.

Magistrates adjourned the case regarding the storeman Henry Provey having to help support the illegitimate child of Mary Ann Weston and then, at a later sitting, agreed that he should pay 2s 6d per week and the usual costs.

The Oddfellows dinner was held at the Bull Inn courtesy of Mrs Gilbert.

At the Lewes County Court James Brooks and James Coleman, executors of the late William Roser, successfully sued Charles Farley for the sum of £8 being the balance for rent.

A health nuisance exists at The Point where pig sties and open cesspools are sited too close to the house. The owner has been given notice again to remedy the problem, otherwise legal proceedings will follow.

The annual meeting of the subscribers to the Chailey Decanal Educational Union was held in Newick this year in the School room with a tent in the School House grounds.

AUGUST 1875

John Langrish's daughter, Emma Jane, died aged 25.

SEPTEMBER 1875

The annual harvest home for about 80 of the labourers from Newick Park was given by J H Sclater, also attended by his 6 sons Robert, Francis, Henry, Arthur, Edward, and Charles. Refreshments, dinner, singing and the obligatory toasts followed. The event included cricket with 20 or 30 players on each side, police constable Robert Buck scoring 30.

The annual Newick Cottagers Show was held at the National School with some fine flowers, vegetables and fruit displayed for judging. All the exhibits were sold at the end of the show. These shows were originally started about 50 years ago by the Rev T Powell with the intention of encouraging good gardening amongst the cottagers.

Each property in the village is assessed to pay a few pence or shillings towards discharging an instalment and interest due on money borrowed for building the wall around the new burial ground.

Another harvest home was held in the two large meadows adjoining The Bull. The day commenced with a procession by the labourers, with the Anscombe Brass Band from Brighton, leading to the church for a service. Dinner was held in a marquee with James Brook from Goldbridge presiding. Cricket followed with the farmers against the tradesmen together with more fun and games – sack races, steeplechase, throwing the cricket ball, dancing, races, etc. W Elphick caused great amusement climbing the greasy pole for a leg of mutton. A thoroughly enjoyable day.

The executors of the will of the late Mr Best Verrall sold various properties – James Petit from Lewes bought 4 cottages and the Rev W Powell bought Snells Field and some cottages. Ivy Lodge facing The Green was bought for £450 by Mr Gravely and the villa next door known as Dickers was bought by Mr Mittens.

OCTOBER 1875

The audit of accounts of the School Board for Newick took place at the Chailey Union Workhouse.

Henry Carvill, a certificated teacher from London, has now taken charge of the National Boys School at a salary of £100 per year.

NOVEMBER 1875

Rain, storm and strong winds brought flooding to the Ouse valley. Dreadful damage occurred along the coast, particularly at Seaford where as many as 49 houses were damaged and families lost furniture, clothing, etc.

DECEMBER 1875

A sad event occurred at William Gilbert's brewery in the High Street – William's brother John, from Fletching, visited with his valuable young retriever who was playing with another dog. Suddenly the retriever jumped into a tub filled with boiling water and was instantly scalded to death.

JANUARY 1876

John Alfred Young, the Colonel's Bank beerhouse keeper, was fined at Petty Sessions in Lewes for being drunk last month in the tap room of his own beerhouse.

Several children are absent from school because of measles and scarlet fever.

Miss Doust has now taken charge of the infants department of the National School, taking over from Miss Bates.

FEBRUARY 1876

The Cuckfield and Haywards Heath Harriers met at the Bull Inn and went for a run with the pack – then all back to the Bull Inn for a dinner courtesy of Mrs Gilbert. Mr Brooks, the farmer, took the chair. Toasts and singing followed with the village string band enlivening the proceedings. Although this is a 10 o'clock district, the magistrates considerately granted an extension of two hours. A merry and convivial evening.

MARCH 1876

Mary Gaston, a 69 year old widow suffering from mental depression, committed suicide. She was found hanging by a cord from the bedstead at her home, Bullfield.

Sarah Ferguson was indecently assaulted at Fount Hill creating great concern in the village.

John Bowden, the master at The National School, died.

APRIL 1876

A £25 reward is now offered to seek the offender for the indecent assault last month.

A large stack of hop baulm was destroyed by fire at Henry Howell's holding, Broomly Farm. Children with matches are supposed to be responsible. A nearby stack was protected by draping it with wet cloths.

Mrs Martha Comber, 30 years at the Royal Oak beerhouse, has been accused of buying beers from other brewers, contrary to the tied house rules. Notice has been served on her to give up possession.

Henry George Avery is now the landlord at The Crown Inn having taken over the licence from Mrs Keeling.

MAY 1876

The Newick Old Friendly Society had its annual church service followed by a dinner, courtesy of Mrs Gilbert, with a band for entertainment. A pleasant afternoon was had by all.

The annual fair was held on The Green.

JUNE 1876

The annual dinner was held at The Zion Chapel.

At the County Court George Norman was successful in claiming £22 10s from William Perkins for failing to pay for a beer delivery.

JULY 1876

The Oddfellows annual fete was held with the usual march to the church, a service by the Rev W Powell and dinner and dancing at the Bull Inn, courtesy of Mrs Gilbert. The Ockenden band played under the direction of Ambrose Dumsday junior. The Lodge is steadily progressing with 98 members in the society.

AUGUST 1876

Stephen Smith, the fruiterer residing at Newick, was near Barcombe Station when his retriever dog found a dead, newly born baby child wrapped in brown paper in a ditch.

The bench of magistrates has transferred the licence for the Bull Inn from Hannah Gilbert to Horatio Stubbs Weston to whom she has recently wed.

The magistrates have agreed a highway rate of 8d in the £ for Newick Parish.

Newick Church (before the 1887 enlargement)

SEPTEMBER 1876

The annual exhibition of the old established Cottage Garden Society was held at The National School Room. Displays from the gentry contributed to the success of the show. The judges included Mr Dicker (gardener to Mrs Archer), Mr W Babbs (gardener to Mrs Blaauw) and Mr Harbour (gardener to Miss Shiffner).

An amateur concert of songs and music was given at The Boys National School Room with performances by W Bates, Miss Kenward, Miss E Fuller, Miss M Pickett, Miss Howell, Miss Gilbert and Miss Bates.

One of the now regular harvest homes was held. A procession of labourers carrying sheaves of wheat, oats, barley etc, and headed by the Anscombe Brass Band from Brighton, marched from the Bull Inn to the church. After the service the party sat down to a fine dinner in a marquee next to the Bull Inn. During the toasts the chairman, J Brook from Goldbridge Farm, denounced the agitations of the Agricultural Union movement and recognised that farmers need not oppress their labourers if those labourers did their duty towards their employers. Sport and entertainment from the band followed in the adjacent field.

OCTOBER 1876

A Mr Luckhurst has been admiring Newick Park and has written an article in the Journal of Horticulture and Cottage Gardener. He praises J H Sclater for the picturesque garden created with alpines, abundant ferns, fine old trees, the beautiful dell and the rock garden – a charming little valley.

An important and influential meeting of landowners was held at the Star Hotel in Lewes to discuss the means of providing a railway line from Lewes to East Grinstead. The Rev W Powell and J H Sclater from Newick attended with the Earl of Sheffield from Sheffield Park as chairman. The idea was discussed 10 years ago when a Railway Bill for creating a line through Newick to Lewes was passed creating great excitement in the village. But that scheme did not get off the ground. Hopefully this latest proposal will have more success.

NOVEMBER 1876

Guy Fawkes night was a fine evening with celebrations better than ever before – processions, the Brighton Town Band, fancy dress and costumes, effigies of guy and the Pope, banners and fireworks.

Lewes Petty Sessions is now forcing Martha Comber to give up possession of the Royal Oak beerhouse.

The Earl of Sheffield attended a meeting of the Board of Directors of the London Brighton and South Coast Railway company to request their co-operation in promoting the building of a railway line between Lewes and East Grinstead. An application is to be made to Parliament for leave to bring in a Bill for building the line including authorisation to take by compulsion the land and houses needed.

DECEMBER 1876

Joseph Staplehurst has been granted a licence as the new tenant at the Royal Oak to replace Martha Comber.

JANUARY 1877

A club supper was held at the Crown Inn with an extension of time allowed by the Petty Sessions.

FEBRUARY 1877

Richard Gravely has provided his annual report (for 1876) for the Chailey Union Rural Sanitary Authority. It records a population of 988 in Newick, with 33 births last year and 17 deaths.

Cuckfield and Haywards Heath Harriers had their annual meet at Newick. After drawing a blank on Mr Hoadley's farm they found a hare on Mr Kennard's land, caught it on Mr Blaauw's estate and despatched it to the Bull Inn to be cooked. Another hare was found on Mr Blaauw's land and chased to Church Farm and to Mr Weston's land but was then lost. The party went back to the Bull Inn for refreshment courtesy of Mr Weston. Afterwards another chase took the party from Goldbridge to Mr John Howells farm, Rotherfield Wood, Newick Wood and back to Goldbridge and the River Ouse. As darkness came on, the hunters finished for the day and went back to the Bull Inn for a fine meal.

The headteacher at the National School was very ill. The managers have employed temporary replacements until a certificated master can be appointed.

MARCH 1877

12 year old Albert Waghorn, a carter boy from Chailey, was ridden over by a wagon and badly injured. He died in Newick Cottage Hospital.

The Earl of Sheffield from Sheffield Park took the oaths and his seat in the House of Lords.

APRIL 1877

John Alfred Young the beerhouse keeper at Colonels Bank was fined ten shillings with thirteen shillings costs for being drunk on his own premises – reminiscent of January last year!

A confirmation service was held at the church by the Lord Bishop of Chichester for the young persons from this and other parishes to receive the sacred rites.

John Smith took charge of the National School.

MAY 1877

The traditional annual fair on the Green is now dwindling badly. This year there was very little livestock on offer.

The Newick Old Benefit Society had its annual event with business at the Bull Inn, a procession with a brass band, a church service, back to the marquee at the Bull Inn for dinner, followed by sports and dancing.

The Newick Cottage Hospital, opened in 1869, produced its seventh annual report. 20 patients were dealt with over the last year with the widow, Mrs Anne Doust, as matron.

JUNE 1877

The anniversary of the 1834 Zion Chapel was well attended.

JULY 1877

Newick played against the Lunatic Asylum at cricket at the Asylum Park. The Asylum Club included four patients.

Officers have been elected for the 'Conservators of the River Ouse' including the Earl of Sheffield and J H Sclater. Mr Sclater recognises that considerable progress has been made in the preservation of the river and that the inspector, Mr Buckland, had reported well on its condition as a salmon river.

The Mid Sussex Lodge of Oddfellows held their annual gathering with a procession to the church for a service and then back to the marquee at the back of the Bull Inn for a dinner courtesy of Mr Weston.

AUGUST 1877

John Alfred Young has now been refused a licence for the Colonels Bank beerhouse.

The Lewes and East Grinstead Railway Bill was read for a third time in the House of Lords and was passed.

SEPTEMBER 1877

A child died of scarlet fever at Vuggles Farm. Doctor Gravely, the Medical Officer of Health, is worried about the spread of infection, particularly as whole families are engaged in hop picking in the nearby hop garden. Also, the cottage itself is very overcrowded with as many as 6 children and 3 adults in just 2 bedrooms.

J H Sclater's second daughter Catherine was married at a grand wedding to Walter F Ingram from Ades, Chailey. Flags, floral decorations and triumphal arches with family crests and mottoes brightened the event. The honeymoon was in Wales.

OCTOBER 1877

Because of the unusual number of deaths this year from hydrophobia Doctor Gravely has seen the need to publicise in the newspaper the symptoms of hydrophobia in dogs – their bark may change, they become fidgety, some will bite every man or beast in their way but others are not ferocious and will gaze about and will lick their owners or lick cold surfaces such as stones or iron. The dogs do not show a fear or dread of water.

NOVEMBER 1877

The railway station for Newick was originally planned to be near Redeens but is now likely to be further away from the village towards Chailey.

Guy Fawkes night was celebrated with the usual vigour after the careful preparations of the Bonfire Boys. The procession included the Newick Fife and Drum Band, coloured lights, clowns, devils, ladies in sixteenth century costumes, ghosts, rockets, tar barrels, a

Nov 3rd Examined the 1st & 3rd Classes in Arithmetic & Dictation. The 1st Class did very well in both subjects with the exception of a few scholars who have been absent for the Summer. The 3rd Class did badly in Arithmetic & the writing was very poor.

I examined also the 4th Class in Arithmetic. Having no help at all progress is very slow here. Decided to give much paper work.

Miss Shiffner visited the School on two occasions & heard the 4th Class read.

Average attendance fr. Week 96·2.

9th The School had a whole holiday on Monday it being "Bonfire Day".

Miss Shiffner visited the School on Tuesday & Thursday & heard the 3rd & 4th Classes read.

The weather has been very wet throughout the Week, consequently the attendance has been much below the average.

Extract from Newick National School log book 1877

flag displaying 'No Popery' and the banner of the Bonfire Boys. The firing of an anvil during the celebrations startled the onlookers.

A fork tailed petrel (a rare bird for Britain) was found dead in a wood near Beechland by Charles Booker. It was sent to Mr Pratt, the naturalist in Brighton, for presentation.

DECEMBER 1877

Ernest Albert Akehurst died aged 13 months from a nut lodged in his throat.

Underwood from Great Rotherfield Wood was for sale at The Griffin, Fletching.

6 or 7 cases of scarlet fever have occurred in the village including the death of 2 children.

John Smith resigned the mastership of the National School.

JANUARY 1878

The National School remained closed after the Christmas holidays because of an outbreak of scarlet fever.

Mr Sclater's cowman, William Knight, committed suicide. Mr Knight's wife found him dead, hanging by the neck from a rope tied to the stair post in the washhouse.

FEBRUARY 1878

The annual hunting gathering assembled at The Crown. The hare was chased through Hangmans Wood, Netherhall, Rotherfield Wood, through Mr Watson's Farm to Sheffield Bridge, Wapsbourne Farm, Wapsbourne Wood, finally catching him after a run of two hours. After a second chase the party returned to The Crown for supper courtesy of Mr Avery with James Brook from Goldbridge, staunch supporter of the hunt, as chairman. Lewes Petty Sessions allowed a one hour extension of opening hours till 11 o'clock.

Edwin W Caws took charge of the National School.

A Valentine card to J H Sclater's daughter Jane

The Chailey Union annual report was presented. Mr Gravely is concerned with the health problem of children, having walked to school in the rain, being obliged to sit in their wet clothes. The school authorities should provide suitable accommodation for changing clothing. It is not surprising that some parents do not always send their children to school on wet days.

condition of those I inspected ; with one or two exceptions the ventilation of the class rooms was very imperfect, and the closet arrangements as inadequate and neglected as when they were before reported on.

It appears by a late return from the Registrar General, that the mean age at death of schoolmasters in England and Wales, is not more than fifty three years, whilst that of adults in various comparatively healthy conditions is sixty five years, we need seek no reason for this, beyond the filthy and un-wholesome atmosphere to which they are often and for so many hours exposed, and this in many instances from their own neglect, in not availing themselves of the means at their disposal for the better ventilation ot the school ; and as a matter of course that which is so pernicious to the health of the teachers is equally so to the scholars ; there is also another defect in our present school system which especially affects the health and comfort of the pupils. Children are now compelled to go to school, and are expected to attend in wet weather as well as fine ; on a wet morning they reach school with their clothes more or less damp, if not saturated with rain, and in this condition they are in most cases doomed to remain for the rest of the day, their clothes slowly drying upon them ; this is what happens to thousands of poor children on every wet morning that the schools are open : surely the school authorities are largely responsible for this condition of things, and as they force parents to send children to school in all weathers, they, on their part should be com-pelled to provide suitable accommodation, where the pupils might change and dry their clothes, and where they could also stow away their extra suit for change : such an arrange-ment would add greatly to the health, comfort and success of the pupils, and at the same time tend to make National and Board Schools more popular with the parents, who, under existing circumstances, would, I think, be morally, if not legally, justified in refusing to send their children to school on a wet day, in spite of what the School Attendance Officer might say to the contrary.

Besides the visits of inspection already mentioned, I have, with the Inspector of Nuisances, made house to house visits at places where such inspection was thought necessary, and I am able to state that so much permanent and substantial sanitary work has now been accomplished in different parts of the district, that house to house visiting is much less necessary than it formerly was. I have, with few exceptions,

Extract from the annual report of the Medical Officer of Health to the Chailey Union Rural Sanitary Authority dated 13th February 1878

MARCH 1878

The survey and trial borings for the proposed new railway line have been made and notices are being served for purchase of the land affected. Daniel Watson's farm to the west of Rotherfield Wood will be directly affected and other land through Chailey Parish will be taken.

Daniel Watson (farmer)

APRIL 1878

The land surveyors and valuers, J Plumer Chapman from Lewes, are advertising their services for settling compensation cases on behalf of landowners affected by the proposed new railway line crossing their land.

S A Dougherty took charge of the National School.

MAY 1878

Mr Wood, the Newick butcher, was at a house near Ditchling Common when his horse bolted and ran through Wivesfield to North Common, Chailey. Past the Kings Head the horse collided with Mr Bannister's pony and cart and overturned it, including the load of groceries and provisions.

The Newick Old Benefit Society had their annual event with a procession, including a brass band, a church service and a dinner at the Bull Inn.

JUNE 1878

Mr Joseph Arch gave an anti-clerical speech on The Green to a gathering of mechanics and labourers.

JULY 1878

The firm, Messrs Pike and Co, from Brighton had a days outing to Newick arriving at the Bull Inn in a four-in-hand and waggonettes. They played cricket with Mr Stead's eleven being bowled out by Bennet and Diplock for a single run! The host Mr Weston catered admirably with the dinner. Toasts were to the success of the firm.

The Mid Sussex Lodge of Oddfellows had their annual event with a procession, including the Anscombes Brighton Brass Band, followed by a church service and then a dinner in a marquee by the Bull Inn and sports.

AUGUST 1878

William Isard the former fellmonger died aged 86 and was buried in the churchyard under the old yew tree.

The pupils of the National School walked to Beechland, through the park, for sports and tea. Mrs Blaauw awarded prizes to those who were distinguished at the Diocesan examinations. The event finished with more refreshments and the National Anthem.

SEPTEMBER 1878

The eighth annual report for the Cottage Hospital issued for 1877 refers to 18 patients being treated, 13 being discharged and one died.

The inmates of the Chailey Union workhouse, young and old, had their days outing travelling on various wagonettes to the Sheffield Arms and Fletching and then coming through Newick. Hearty cheers were given to them all along the route. They then continued back to the workhouse for a roast beef and plum pudding dinner, entertainments including a magic lantern with dissolving views and the Gilbert family from Newick providing music. The day finished with dancing and praise to the workhouse master and matron.

OCTOBER 1878

A suicide has created gloom over the village. William Sumner Smith from Golden Point shot himself in the mouth with a five chambered revolver. Mr Gravely attended and PC Buck, the Newick constable, informed the coroner. The poor man had been a cheerful and genial gentleman and a follower of the Southdown foxhounds.

About 150 people attended a National Labourers Union meeting on The Green addressed by a Mr Dickens and a Mr Tatton, delegates from the Executive Council. The talk was on the need for land reform to give more benefits to the labouring classes.

Doctor Gravely provided a report to the Chailey Union on the sanitary conditions of schools in the district. The Newick National School is satisfactory with suitable lavatories, earth closets and fine ventilation to the large classroom. The Lady Vernon School requires a syphon ventilator and the closets need daily attendance.

NOVEMBER 1878

The contract for building the new railway line has been awarded to Joseph Firbank from Newport, Monmouthshire, requiring the line to be completed ready for inspection by the Board of Trade by July 1880.

The well attended Guy Fawkes celebrations were held with a procession headed by two residents on horseback. The village Drum and Fife Band under the leadership of Mr Brooks followed, together with a 'No Popery' banner and the marchers in costumes. The route went to the houses of the gentry where gifts were received and then back for the lighting of the bonfire. The guy and Pope effigies were burnt, tar barrels set alight, rockets, squibs and crackers set off and the evening finishing with 'God Save the Queen'.

Henry Eastland was charged with stealing rabbits from Richard Fuller and also from Joseph Staplehurst the occupier of the Royal Oak beerhouse.

DECEMBER 1878

The annual dinner for the cottagers and employees of the Beechlands estate was given by Mrs Blaauw – roast beef, plum pudding and more. Mrs Blaauw passed her best wishes for a happy Christmas and each man received a ½ pound packet of tea as a present. Health was drunk to Mrs Blaauw followed by music, God Save the Queen and then home.

JANUARY 1879

There has been considerable flooding in the County including in the Ouse valley.

Huts are to be erected shortly at Lane End Common to accommodate the workers who will be building the new railway line through Newick and Chailey.

A club supper was held at the Crown Inn.

The vestry meeting considered making an application to the County Authority that several roads in the Parish should become main roads, namely the road from the post office/telegraph office to Golden Point, the road from Bushy Plat near Newick Park to the proposed railway station and the road from Goldbridge to Golden Point, which was the turnpike prior to 1870.

FEBRUARY 1879

Work has started on building the new railway line. Several hundred more navvies are expected locally when their temporary accommodation huts are completed. Mr Kenward has lent a team of horses to assist the contractor.

THE NEW RAILWAY.—The work for the new Lewes and Eastgrinstead railway has commenced in this parish, and will be prosecuted with vigour. Boring for clay for making bricks shows a prospect of an abundant supply. Metals are being laid for draught purposes, and when the contemplated building of huts is completed, an additional immigration of two or three hundred navvies may be expected. It is, we are informed, almost universally regretted in the neighbourhood that it has been found necessary to alter the site of the proposed station. The original plan placed it near Reeden's, on the main and most frequented road between Chailey and Newick, but the impracticability of the site for a luggage station, on account of a declivity, has led to the determination to erect it at Ox Bottom, about a mile further distant from these villages. This change, however, will necessitate the m.cadamising of a new approach, and be a source of greater inconvenience to pedestrians.

Newaspaper cutting on the building of the railway – February 1879

MARCH 1879

The annual hunt took place. A hare was found at Beechland but the hounds were called off. Another was found at Little Rotherfield Wood and chased through Lane End, Wet Wood, Rotherfield, Great Wood, Hangmans Rough, Goldbridge and finishing bloodless at Founthill Wood. Another hare was found and then the day was rounded off with dinner and traditional toasts at the Bull Inn.

An annual collection was held at the National School on behalf of the Teachers Orphanage and Orphan Fund.

APRIL 1879

At the vestry meeting overseers were elected. Richard Gravely and John Howell were chosen as churchwardens.

The 6-bedroom house 'The Point' is to let with stable, harness room, coach house, cow house, piggery etc.

Her Majesty's inspectors visited the National School.

There was a good supply of cattle at the Newick Fair where a reasonable amount of business was done. Job Smith, the Lewes horse dealer, was badly kicked in the abdomen by a horse.

MAY 1879

Petty Sessions in Lewes considered a request for providing a special constable for Newick, particularly because there are now so many navvies here – about 86 in Newick as well as others in Chailey, Barcombe etc.

The Brighton Snowdrops, a celebrated minstrel group, provided music, songs and jokes to a packed National School Room.

The Friendly Society meeting was held at the Bull Inn in the usual manner.

JUNE 1879

A middle aged man at Newick Park is offering his services in a newspaper advertisement as a farm bailiff. The advertisement states that he thoroughly understands management of farming, hops, corn, seeds, breeding and rearing of stock and sheep and that his wife is a good dairy and poultry woman.

Some of the contractors staff with a saddletank locomotive
at Lane End Common during the construction of the new railway line.

JULY 1879

Dr Gravely visited the National School and suggests that the infants classroom needs better ventilation. The Lady Vernon School also requires a syphon ventilator.

At only 19 years of age, Arthur William Bassett Sclater appeared in the score books for Sussex County Cricket in a match against the 'Anomalies'.

The Hand and Heart Club had its gathering in the field next to the Bull Inn with a dinner together with a band from Cuckfield. Unfortunately frequent showers marred the day.

AUGUST 1879

A thatched storage building at William Gilbert's brewery caught fire, probably by a spark from the brewery chimney. The building was destroyed with some damage to the brewery and malthouse. Fire engines from Uckfield and Sheffield Park were called but the fire was under control before they arrived.

A stoolball match was held in James Brook's field together with tea for about 120 people. The Newick band provided dance music in the evening. Kiss-in-the-ring and other amusements brought the proceedings to an end.

SEPTEMBER 1879

There have been outbreaks of scarlet fever in the village. Dr Gravely has given instructions on appropriate disinfecting, cleaning and whitewashing to control infection.

The Cottagers Garden show in the School Room was a success with displays of fruit, vegetables and flowers.

James Lewis, a navvy at Newick, has been remanded for stealing 1s 6d from his mate.

OCTOBER 1879

A rate of 8d in the £ will be charged for relief of the poor in the Parish. 228 properties have been listed for assessment.

A meeting in Lewes attended by T St Leger Blaauw, Richard Gravely, Rev W Powell and others set up a Committee to try to resurrect the building of a railway line between Sheffield Bridge and Hellingly. The route, following through the Parish of Newick, was partly built but then abandoned. The Brighton Railway Company will be approached.

S A Doughty gave up charge of the National School.

The Cottage Hospital produced its 9th annual report. The needs of the workers on the new railway line makes this local hospital increasingly important.

NOVEMBER 1879

Thomas Jones took charge of the National School.

The Guy Fawkes celebrations were on a far less grand scale than usual this year because there are so many railway navvies living near the village and many of the leading gentry in the neighbourhood have therefore held back their subscriptions. Nevertheless the school boys procured some fuel for a bonfire, paraded the streets and a few fireworks were discharged.

At his rent audit J H Sclater from Newick Park has agreed to return 10% of the half-yearly rent to his tenants.

The Inspector of Nuisances, together with Dr Gravely, visited most of the houses in Newick. Some properties have inadequate cesspools, untrapped drains, drains too close to wells etc but generally, little needs attention in terms of public health and sanitation.

DECEMBER 1879

The local gentry have provided a reading room close to the railway navvies huts near the High Road from Chailey, for the benefit of the navvies. It will have newspapers etc and is intended to keep the navvies out of mischief.

Mrs Blaauw provided the annual dinner at Beechlands for the cottagers. Each cottager was presented with a half pound packet of tea. Music and the National Anthem concluded the event.

After six weeks of inactivity because of frosts the Southdown Foxhounds assembled at Longford Bridge. The fox was chased to Newick Park, Piltdown, Fletching and north to Searles.

Police Constable Robert Buck found Mark Newnham, the labourer from Fletching, drunk and disorderly. At court Newnham was fined 5 shillings and 5 shillings costs.

George Murrell was fined £5 10s 0d including costs for being drunk and refusing to leave the Bull Inn when requested to do so.

Mrs M E Blaauw of Beechlands

JANUARY 1880

The Southdown Foxhounds met at Chailey village and found a fox on William Uridge's land. It was chased to Gipps Wood, to Mr Shenstone's estate, on to Longford Bridge, through Newick Park and finally went to ground back in Gipps Wood.

FEBRUARY 1880

A concert of vocals and instrumental music was held at the National School in aid of the funds for the recently built Railway Reading Room.

The fox hunt from the Old Ship at Plashett chased the fox through Newick Old Park to The Point and up to The Warren and Chailey Common. A gentleman from Kemp Town, Brighton jumped straight into the middle of the river, on his horse, and had to swim ashore.

MARCH 1880

The teacher, Miss Doust, at the National School has been suspended from duty.

The annual hare hunt was held.

APRIL 1880

Thomas Thompson, formerly of Newick, was given 6 months hard labour for stealing £83 last June from Joseph Firbank the contractor on the new railway line.

MAY 1880

21 year old Arthur William Bassett Sclater played cricket for Sussex at Lords against an M C C side.

J H Sclater has reduced the half-yearly rent for his tenants by 10%.

JUNE 1880

Owing to failing health W Horscraft has to give up his baker and corn dealer business in Newick which he has run for the last 37 years. Richard Hayler is to take over.

A railway navvy was found dead on a bank in a field near Cinder Hill railway cutting.

The Newick choir boys played the National School boys at cricket.

JULY 1880

Another death has occurred on the railway. An 18 year old, Richard Daws, fell through the bridge over the Lewes to East Grinstead road. He and two others were walking down the line in the evening and he was probably jumping across the open girders of the bridge, as a bit of bravado, and missed his footing. William C Faber, the civil engineer from The Point, Newick and agent for the railway contractor, assisted in giving evidence at the inquest.

A PLEA FOR NAVVIES.—Mrs Kingsley (the widow of the late Mr H. Kingsley, novelist), writing from Cuckfield to a London contemporary, says :—" I am a constant visitor to the infirmary of the Union for a large number of parishes. Recently men have been brought, mainly navvies, in such an advanced state of disease that they are past human aid. Who is to blame? Surely when railway or other works are in course of construction some more adequate accommodation than over-crowded huts, or even more over-crowded farmhouses and cottages ought to be provided by the contractors ; and wherever the men are massed together there ought to be at least a bi-weekly medical inspection, in order to ascertain whether there are cases of illness or not, and not to be left to the chance of any one sending for a doctor." The lady mentions several cases, and adds :—" When we consider that these men aid us, forming as it were a bridge of their lives, to enable us to reach those whom we love, and hear their dying words, and receive their last look, we ought to feel bound to succour them, so far as possible, from dying alone and amongst strangers in a workhouse infirmary."

Newspaper cutting on the plight of railway navvies – July 1880

Charles Douch, the Newick wheelwright, pleaded guilty at Petty Sessions to being drunk and disorderly and was fined 1 shilling with 3 shillings costs.

AUGUST 1880

A young navvy, 20 year-old John Sheppard, was killed on the railway line. He was a rope runner engaged in uncoupling the trucks but this time he got in between the trucks before they had finished bumping and was badly injured. He died in Newick Cottage Hospital.

A Sunday School has started for the children of the railway workers.

A scuffle occurred at the Bricklayers Arms when John Staplehurst was hit about the face after he refused to lend sixpence to Philip Hodge.

SEPTEMBER 1880

Because of Richard Gravely's severe and protracted illness with rheumatism the annual report for the Rural Sanitary Authority of the Chailey Union has only just been published.

A well attended entertainment was provided at the Railway Reading Room for the men employed in constructing the new railway line. Performances were given by Mrs Hilton, Mrs Banks, Mrs Greenway and the pupils of Miss Swaysland's school with vocals and instrumentals.

OCTOBER 1880

There was a very large attendance at another successful show for the railway workers at the Railway Reading Room. Performances were given by Miss Fuller, the pupils of the Swaysland School and others.

Five of George Fenner's heifers were found wandering in the roadway.

A party was held in the Railway Reading Room for the Sunday School children of the railway workers followed by sports, races and football.

NOVEMBER 1880

The licence for the Bricklayers Arms beerhouse has been transferred from Thomas Evans to Benjamin Turner. John Staplehurst has taken over the licence for the Royal Oak from Joseph Staplehurst.

An industrial exhibition was held at the Reading Room.

A local navvy, James Williams, was given 6 weeks hard labour at Lewes Petty Sessions for stealing a pair of stockings and handkerchief from Henry Budgen and 2 tame rabbits from James Wheatland. PC Robert Buck had apprehended him. Williams had told PC Buck that he had slept under the railway bridge at Cinder Hill and, when he awoke in the morning, the 2 rabbits were by his side. The magistrate was not impressed with this story.

A sale of underwood took place at Newick Park.

Another thoroughly enjoyable programme of entertainment was given for the railway workers at the Reading Room, including a handbell performance by the Brooks family.

A labourer, John Eastland, stole 2 gallons of barley from William Stephens and sold it to a ganger at the railway huts. He has been sent to gaol for 6 weeks.

DECEMBER 1880

A navvy, William Davis, was found so drunk on the road from Newick to Chailey that special constable Anscombe had to take him to the police station in a hand-cart. He was fined.

Charles Horscroft and Mark Newnham have been charged with being drunk and refusing to quit a licenced premises at Newick.

JANUARY 1881

With the prolonged Arctic weather and lying snow the railway navvies have been unable to work and are now suffering distress and hunger and are becoming desperate. Many roads in Sussex are blocked. After one great snowstorm The Duchess of Norfolk and her maid were even obliged to spend the night in the waiting room of Lewes station.

The Rev A C MacLaglan was presented with a very handsome gold watch by the friends and navvies of Newick in great appreciation of the good work he has done over the last 9 months in the welfare of the railway workers. He is about to leave to do missionary work in Africa. His kind and genial manner was welcomed and he will be much missed.

FEBRUARY 1881

The Rev A C MacLaglan has received more farewell gifts, this time from Miss Swaysland and her pupils at the Newick Green Seminary – drawings, a cushion, a fancy bag, a wool anti-macassar, table mats etc.

MARCH 1881

Arthur Sclater is to go to Virginia, America to an agricultural business. As a batsman and bowler he will be missed by the Sussex County Cricket Club.

APRIL 1881

The 10-yearly National Census was held this month counting all the Parish population and recording their jobs – agricultural labourers, journeymen, domestic servants, maids, grooms, coachmen, stablemen, gardeners, laundry workers, dressmakers, shoemakers, butchers, fellmongers, carpenters, builders, blacksmiths, carriers etc. There were a lot more people in Newick to count this time with over 40 railway construction navvies including their families in lodgings plus more than 30 in the temporary railway huts.

The infants part of the National School closed. A new infants school will need to be provided.

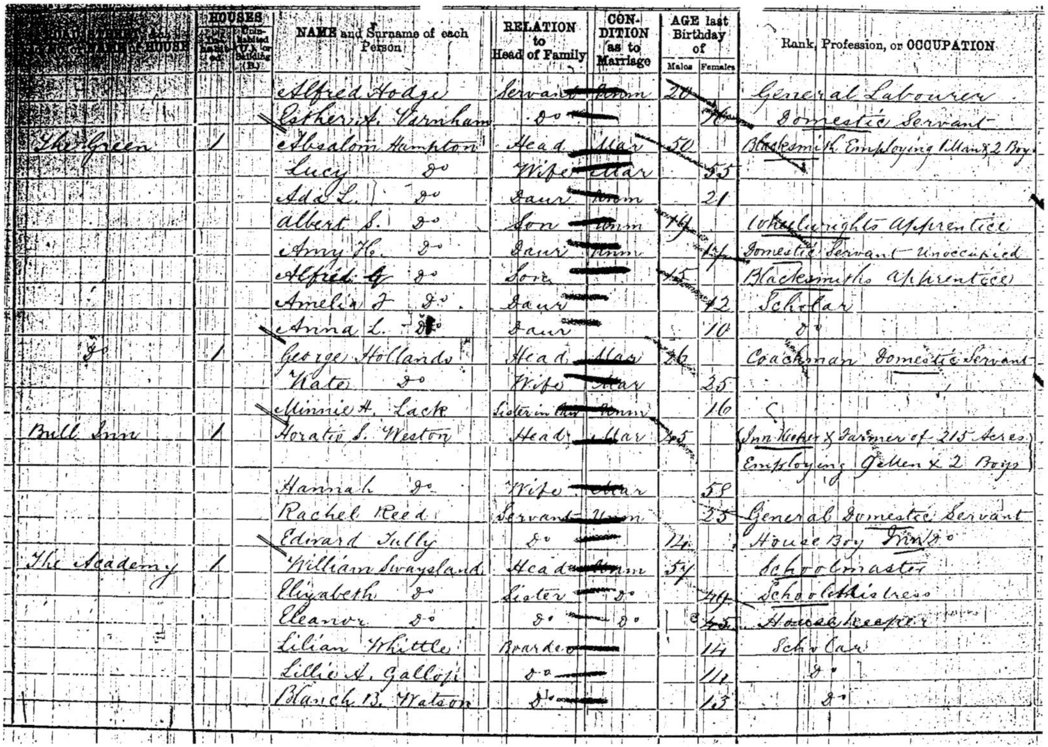

Road, Street, &c., and No. or Name of House	Houses Inhabited	Houses Uninhabited (U.), or Building (B.)	NAME and Surname of each Person	RELATION to Head of Family	CONDITION as to Marriage	AGE last Birthday of Males	AGE last Birthday of Females	Rank, Profession, or OCCUPATION
			Alfred Hodge	Servant	Unm	20		General Labourer
			Esther A. Varnham	do			16	Domestic Servant
The Green	1		Absalom Hampton	Head	Mar	50		Blacksmith Employing 1 Man & 2 Boys
			Lucy do	Wife	Mar		55	
			Ada L. do	Daur	Unm		21	
			Albert S. do	Son	Unm	19		Wheelwrights Apprentice
			Amy H. do	Daur	Unm		17	Domestic Servant Unoccupied
			Alfred G. do	Son		15		Blacksmiths Apprentice
			Amelia J. do	Daur			12	Scholar
			Anna L. do	Daur			10	do
do	1		George Hollands	Head	Mar	26		Coachman Domestic Servant
			Kate do	Wife	Mar		25	
			Minnie A. Lack	Sister in Law	Unm		16	
Bull Inn	1		Horatio S. Weston	Head	Mar	45		Inn Keeper & Farmer of 215 Acres Employing 9 Men & 2 Boys
			Hannah do	Wife	Mar		58	
			Rachel Reed	Servant	Unm		23	General Domestic Servant
			Edward Tully	do		14		House Boy Inn do
The Academy	1		William Swaysland	Head	Unm	54		Schoolmaster
			Elizabeth do	Sister	do		40	Schoolmistress
			Eleanor do	do	do		45	Housekeeper
			Lilian Whittle	Boarder			14	Scholar
			Lillie A. Gallop	do			14	do
			Blanch B. Watson	do			13	do

Extract from the 1881 census returns

MAY 1881

Thomas Jones, the National School master, has been updating the school register which, prior to his taking over the school in November 1879, had been inadequately kept for many months. He is in dispute with the Rev William Powell over payment for the extra work. The County Court at Lewes heard the case but disallowed Mr Jones' claim for payment because there had been no actual contract between him and the school managers.

The annual fair was held on The Green with cattle and sheep but not much business was done. Showers finished the day off.

A young man was badly injured on the railway. He was pressed between the buffers while hooking on the couplings.

JUNE 1881

The Inspector of Nuisances has reported on the various sanitation problems in the village including The Bricklayers Arms where the closet is sited too close to the house.

Mr Blencowe retired as treasurer for the Cottage Hospital, a post which he has held since the hospital was created in 1869. Mr Blaauw will replace him. The hospitals annual report shows that 23 cases have been dealt with over the year. The institution has provided a valuable service to those injured or sick workers on the railway line now under construction. The railway workers have contributed helpful subscriptions to the hospital.

The Boys School closed for a while for want of a master. Thomas Jones has given up charge of the school in some discontent with the managers.

JULY 1881

22 year old John Oldaker took charge of the National School.

The Mid Sussex Lodge of Oddfellows had their annual church service at Newick followed by a feast in a marquee by the Bull Inn. The Lewes Volunteer and Town Band provided music. The feast was followed by sports.

Extract from an article entitled 'Sussex Folk and Sussex Ways' by the Rev. John Coker Egerton, rector of Burwash, Sussex – in 'Leisure Hour' magazine July 1881.

safely enough, and though the ghost had vanished it had taken the boots with it.

The following instance of mixed ideas about this world and another, I look upon as very exceptional, though it comes to me from the tradesman who was serving the funeral in Newick parish at which it occurred. In the ordinary course, he asked the woman who was attending the funeral party for the registrar's certificate of death. "Do you mean the ticket, sir?" she said. "Yes," he replied, "the ticket." "Oh, sir," said the woman, "I put that in the box (*i.e.*, the coffin); I thought the poor soul might want it when he got to heaven." I should have been curious to trace the origin of this idea, as it has no parallel in my Sussex experience. I have never actually known more than one person who

AUGUST 1881

The boys of the National School had their treat at Beechlands courtesy of Mrs Blaauw with sports, tea and prize books for the 18 boys who were successful in the scripture examination.

SEPTEMBER 1881

The executors of the late Edward Stephens held an auction for the farming stock of Painters Farm including two draught horses, a gelding, two dairy cows, a calf, a hog, waggons, carts, rollers, harrows, a plough, tools, household furniture etc.

OCTOBER 1881

Evening classes commenced at the National School with six scholars attending.

NOVEMBER 1881

James Herbert, a railway navvy, was jailed for 14 days for refusing to leave The Bricklayers Arms, for assaulting Benjamin Turner the landlord and for breaking a pane of glass.

North Lodge is to let. It has 5 bedrooms, 3 servants bedrooms, a gardeners cottage, stables, coach house, lawn tennis ground and paddock.

DECEMBER 1881

Timber from the Newick Park Estate was sold at the Bull Inn.

JANUARY 1882

The new Lewes to East Grinstead railway line is now nearly completed except for the stations.

The Newick Park Harriers met at Pinnacle Pit. A good hunting run of 45 minutes took place through the Park, over the river to Bushy Plat, Park House, School house, Double Barns, Bushy Plat pit, down over the river, Plain Park, and down to the pond for the final kill of the hare.

Ellen Eddis has been found guilty of stealing a horse rug from Mr Weston at The Bull Inn and will be imprisoned for one month plus hard labour.

FEBRUARY 1882

Mr Gravely's annual report to the Chailey Union Rural Sanitary Authority was presented for the year 1881. In regard to Newick it refers to scattered cases of measles, one death from croup and one death from erysipelas.

The evening school held at the National School has now closed because of insufficient numbers of scholars.

MARCH 1882

The Earl of Sheffield, J St Leger Blaauw and very many others are becoming increasingly concerned about the delays in opening the new railway line.

Allen Anscombe, the carrier who operated between Lewes and Chailey died and was buried in Newick churchyard.

A sad suicide case has occurred – Rosina Baker from Oxbottom cut her own throat and died at The Sussex County Hospital.

Golden Cottage has been bought by T St Leger Blaauw for £200 and two tenements on The Green, occupied by Alfred Coppard and John Vinall, have been bought for £515 by H G Avery.

APRIL 1882

Horatio Stubbs Weston, the licensed victualer and farmer, is in dispute with the Newick overseers for not paying the poor rate and the highway rate levied on him in respect of Ketches Farm and the farmhouse. The farmhouse has remained unlet since October 1881 so Mr Weston is unwilling to pay that part of the rate although happy to pay for the farm. The magistrate considered that powers exist for the farm and the farmhouse to be assessed separately and so declined to make an order to force Mr Weston to pay the whole sum.

MAY 1882

Gipps Farm with its 110 acres is to let.

The village fair was held on The Green.

The church weathervane is dated 1882

The Inspector of Nuisances has drawn attention to sanitation problems at various properties including The Royal Oak Inn, the shop on The Green and Alfred Hemsley's house.

The annual club day was held in the village.

JUNE 1882

James Miles is now the landlord at The Crown Inn.

J H Sclater's fourth son, Arthur W B Sclater, died aged 22, in an accident whilst duck shooting in New Zealand. He had rendered good service to Sussex cricket.

Arthur William Bassett Sclater
(1859-1882)

The executors of the late John Pickett sold two copyhold properties. Lot 1 was Yew Villa, a four bedroom, detached cottage including well, piggeries, fruit trees etc sold to Mr Gurr for £305. Lot 2 was 3, Western Road, a cottage in two tenements opposite the Zion Chapel, sold to Mr Cookson for £420.

The house known as The Point is to let, unfurnished, including the stables, harness room, coach house, cow house, piggeries, gardeners cottage and 4 acres.

North Lodge is to let with its 5 bedrooms, 3 servants rooms, a gardeners cottage, stables, coach house and lawn tennis ground.

JULY 1882

Thomas Henty, carter to Mr John Howell of Church Farm, had a bad accident near The Crown Inn. His horse bolted and Thomas was ran over by the wagon, breaking his leg.

The Board of Trade inspector Colonel Yollond inspected the new railway line to see if it is satisfactory for opening. At Newick station (where the first brick was laid by the Newick bricklayer John Brooks) Colonel Yollond says that some stop blocks are needed at the ends of the sidings, the catch points need to be prolonged and another urinal is required. He is impressed with Saxby and Farmers signalling arrangements. Overall it is a "very well finished line". There have been some heavy slips on some of the deep embankments so he warns that they will have to be carefully looked after.

AUGUST 1882

The new railway line was finally opened at last on a delightfully fine day. The children from Newick School had a half day holiday and enjoyed waving at the train from the bridge. The stationmaster at Newick and Chailey station is William Mullinger who has previously been employed at Cooksbridge Station. The timetable is 5 trains per day for passenger traffic linking Newick with Lewes, Brighton and East Grinstead. Timothy Watson and Louisa Freeland were two of those that travelled on the first train from the new station.

70 children attended the annual National School treat at Beechlands.

SEPTEMBER 1882

The Gulcher Electric Light and Power Co Ltd intend to apply to the Board of Trade for a provisional order authorizing the supply of electricity for public and private purposes within the District of Chailey.

The new railway station with the stationmaster, his staff and some workmen

51

The 12th anniversary of the opening of the Cottage Hospital was celebrated with a church service followed by tea at the National School.

OCTOBER 1882

A new school for infants (boys and girls) has now been opened by James Sclater next to the Lady Vernons charity girls school. It has cost about £350 to build. Being a very wet opening day, only 2 pupils attended! E V Uridge is the temporary teacher until the appointed certificated teacher starts in December.

William Mullinger, the stationmaster, has been presented with a handsome silver watch by his friends for his work at Cooksbridge station.

There has been an earth slip on the new railway line about one mile to the south of Newick and Chailey station. Colonel Yollond, the Board of Trade inspector, had warned in July that these banks would need to be looked after.

NOVEMBER 1882

Attendance at the new infants school is slowly increasing.

A concert was held in the National School to raise funds for the school.

DECEMBER 1882

Newick police constable Robert Buck was awarded a handsome silver watch and a purse of money by 92 inhabitants of Newick for his service over the last 15 years. He is moving to Rotherfield.

Kate Sadler, the new certificated teacher, has started her duties at the new infants school.

W C Faber, the civil engineer from The Point, is leaving Newick so he has had a sale of his household furniture and effects.

JANUARY 1883

An accident occurred at the railway station. The train from East Grinstead to Brighton ran into the sidings in darkness by mistake and hit the buffers. The locomotive was damaged. The 23 year old fireman, Mr J George, was injured and taken to the Cottage Hospital.

17 year old Thomas Callaway, a pupil teacher, was accidentally shot and killed by his brother in Mr Dumsday's garden at 2, Western Road. Doctor Gravely attended.

The Burstow Hunt met at Fletching with a fine pack of hounds which chased the hare from Sir Spencer Wilson's covers at Netherhall Farm, through Guns Wood, Goldbridge Farm and on to Piltdown and The Rocks.

The chairman of the School Board for the Parish, J H Sclater, is concerned that the National School is taking back some infants despite there now being a separate infant school.

The Walford family, comprising 5 youthful brothers and sisters, visited Newick on their tour of south-east England and gave a fine display of bell-ringing using 102 bells. The large and appreciative audience enjoyed the music, recitations and songs.

A concert of songs and music in the Boys School room was performed almost exclusively by people from Newick.

FEBRUARY 1883

During the current spell of bad weather, with the lull in farm work, labourers are being kept well employed on large ornamental works in the grounds of the gentry.

Serious floods have affected much of East Sussex.

MARCH 1883

In Doctor Gravely's annual report to the Chailey Union, Newick is considered to be, on the whole, in a better state than it was a few years ago in regard to health and sanitation.

APRIL 1883

The Education Department has criticised the new infants school opened last October with its unsuitable benches, dirty walls with no pictures of animals, inadequate playground and Mary Pearce, the unclassified teacher, being less than efficient.

The annual livestock fair on The Green was better attended than for some time although sales were not very brisk.

MAY 1883

Richard Gravely's son Frank has received his diploma and has been admitted as a member of the Royal College of Surgeons.

A Mr John Best was walking along the railway line to the south of Sheffield Park station, as a short cut route, when the Lewes to East Grinstead passenger train struck him and fractured his skull, killing him instantly. His two companions escaped injury.

The School Board says that Miss Kate Sadler, at the infants school, deserves great praise.

JUNE 1883

The Newick Friendly Society had its annual dinner at the Bull Inn together with a church service.

JULY 1883

A correspondent in the newspaper suggests that the prospects for hop growers have never been better. There are now 21½ acres of hops in the Parish.

About 3,000 people watched the cricket match at Sheffield Park between Lord Sheffield's XI and Doctor W G Grace's XI.

The Sunday School children and the church choir boys had a trip to Crystal Palace.

AUGUST 1883

The wife of J H Sclater died of internal cancer aged 58. She had taken a great interest in all the Parochial institutions and was especially active in promoting the welfare of the village schools. On the day of the funeral from mid-day until after the internment, nearly every blind in the village was drawn in respect. There were about 200 mourners at the graveside.

The boys of the National School and the children of the village infant school had their annual treat at Beechland with amusements, tea and scripture prizes. The day finished with the National Anthem and three cheers for Mr and Mrs Blaauw.

SEPTEMBER 1883

Severe gales and storms hit Sussex.

At the annual Cottagers Show in the decorated school room the number and quality of exhibits of flowers, fruit and vegetables was above average. Lunch was provided for the judges and officials in one of the classrooms. In the evening about 300 people paid for admission to see the displays.

At Lewes Petty Sessions James Coleman was fined for assaulting his wife and also bound over in the sum of £10 to keep the peace for 6 months.

OCTOBER 1883

An outbreak of scarlet fever closed the schools for a while. Dr Gravely suggests that the source may have been the children working in the neighbouring hop gardens.

James Miles, the landlord of The Crown Inn, was badly injured when he was thrown from a horse that he was breaking in. Dr Gravely had to treat his head wound with stitches.

J H Sclater organised the annual harvest home at Newick Park for his estate workers with a dinner, cricket and tea.

The girls from the Lady Vernons School and the children from the infants school visited Newick Park for amusements, a dinner in the coach house and tea together with singing and presents for each child. It is 100 years ago this year that James Lambert, the distinguished painter from Lewes, did paintings of the mansion at Newick Park and the Lady Vernon school.

The International Fisheries Exhibition at South Kensington, London has been a popular excursion with 96 tickets being issued for the cheap Thursday train from Newick and Chailey station.

An auction was held at Tilehouse Farm for the sale of stock and effects including two horses, a waggon, a dung cart, a winnowing machine, a harness, poultry etc.

NOVEMBER 1883

The Guy Fawkes celebrations were on a grand scale this year despite the damp weather and the lack of a band. About 60 masqueraders joined the torchlight procession with two or three amusing effigies as caricatures of local celebrities. Chinese lanterns were suspended from many houses. Guy Fawkes and the Pope were burnt on the huge bonfire on The Green and a firework display was provided. Another bonfire was provided at Beechlands with fireworks.

Frank Gravely, eldest son of Richard Gravely and now a partner in his father's practice, married Miss Kate Boxall at Wisborough Green. The honeymoon will be in Torquay.

The Coal Club offered a 5s bonus this year.

DECEMBER 1883

Collections from the harvest thanksgiving services at Newick, Chailey and Scaynes Hill have raised £28 6s 5½d for the Cottage Hospital.

The Southdown foxhounds met at Chailey and chased the fox around the countryside including through Newick Park, killing him at Longford Bridge.

A meeting was held at the Bull Inn with R Gravely in the chair to ascertain what steps could be taken to form a new cricket club for the village. The old cricket club was formed in February 1871. A Committee was appointed to find a suitable ground for matches and practice.

NEWICK.

PROPOSED CRICKET CLUB.—A meeting was held at the Bull in on Friday evening for the purpose of ascertaining what steps could be taken to form a cricket club in the village. Mr. R. Gravely occupied the chair and there was a very fair attendance. After some discussion a committee was appointed to make enquires whether a suitable ground can be obtained for practice and matches, there being no such place available at present.

Newspaper cutting on proposed cricket club – December 1883

JANUARY 1884

W Martin, the local builder and Parish Clerk for many years, died aged 66.

56 year old George Ball, the former coachman to the Rev William Powell, was found hanged in his closet. He was cut down by Vince Wood and his neighbour the wheelwright George Henry Chrismas. He had been afflicted by paralysis.

Mr and Mrs Sturt celebrated their 61st wedding anniversary. Mrs Sturt, aged 81, was for 35 years the mistress at the Lady Vernon girls school.

FEBRUARY 1884

Philip Hodge, a labourer from Newick, has been fined 5 shillings with 10 shillings costs at Lewes Petty Sessions for being drunk and disorderly.

The minstrel troupe 'The Brighton Snowdrops' gave a performance of jokes and songs at the National Schoolroom.

MARCH 1884

falling downstairs.—The jury returned a verdict in accordance with the medical evidence.

CRICKET CLUB.—An adjourned meeting was held at the Bull Inn, on Thursday evening for the purpose of forming a Cricket Club. Mr R. Gravely occupied the chair, and there was a very good attendance, including Messrs F. Gravely, J. Oldaker, A. Tidy, Potter, Humphrey, M. Wood, J. Brook, jun., Hemsley, &c., &c. The Committee appointed at the last meeting reported that the landlord of the Bull Inn had kindly offered to let to the Cricket Club, rent free, the field adjoining the inn ; and on the recommendation of the Committee the ground was accepted, the Club undertaking to put it in a fit state to play on. Rules were then formed, about thirty members were enrolled, and the following officers were appointed : President, T. St. Leger Blaauw, Esq. ; captain and treasurer, Mr Frank Gravely ; secretary, Mr J. Oldaker; committee, R. Gravely, Esq., Messrs Potter, Humphrey, M. Wood, A. Tidy, and Aemsley. Further arrangements as to matches were left to be carried out by the Committee.

Newspaper cutting on proposed cricket club – March 1884

At a meeting at the Bull Inn a new cricket club for Newick was formed with about 30 members enrolling. Club rules were agreed. The landlord kindly offered rent free, the use of the field adjoining the Inn. Hopefully the old cricket club may provide some materials. The president of the club will be T St Leger-Blaauw, the captain and treasurer Frank Gravely, the secretary J Oldaker and the committee will be R Gravely, Mr Potter, Mr Humphrey, Mr Wood, Mr Hemsley and Mr A Tidy.

APRIL 1884

Kate Sadler gave up charge of the infants school. Elizabeth S Bayliss has now taken over.

The annual fair on The Green was well attended this year with more livestock for sale than usual and plenty of amusements later in the day. The Fletching Brass Band helped to enliven the proceedings.

Thomas Waters is the new licence holder at The Bull Inn.

MAY 1884

The schoolchildren had a half day holiday for May Day celebrations.

Lord Sheffield held a cricket match at Sheffield Park between an All-England eleven and the Australian cricketers. The children of the National School were given a day's holiday.

15 children over 6 years of age were dismissed from the infants school in accordance with the requirements of the School Board. These older children should be educated at the boys school or at Lady Vernons.

The 13th annual report of the Cottage Hospital shows that this institution is in a satisfactory condition.

About 80 sat down to the dinner of the Old Benefit Society in a marquee at the Bull Inn courtesy of the host Mr Waters. The Fletching Band played for the dancing.

The newly formed Newick Cricket Club had an eventful start. In the game at Sheffield Park 54 year old John Gilbert scored 250 not out for Fletching.

JUNE 1884

The 50th anniversary of the Zion Baptist Chapel was held with services, mid-day dinner and tea.

J H Sclater's third son Captain Henry Crichton Sclater married Miss Edith Harriett Barttelot at Stopham church near Pulborough. The honeymoon was in the Isle of Wight. Captain Sclater will then go to Egypt where his regiment is quartered.

The first home match of the recently formed Newick Cricket Club was played against the Chailey club. The team was A Bates, J Brook, R Fuller, F Gravely, A Hemsley, W J Martin, J Oldaker, A Osborn, F Potter, A Tidy and M Wood. Newick won by 6 runs, J Brook playing a fine innings. Lunch was provided by Mr Waters from the Bull Inn.

Kate Sadler, the former teacher at the infants school, is now married to William Luckins.

JULY 1884

Newick played against Fletching in the return cricket match at Sheffield Park. John Gilbert was again in fine form for Fletching using a new bat which was presented to him by the Earl of Sheffield who was distinctly impressed with his score of 250 not out in the last match between Newick and Fletching. He has also been awarded a silver plaque for his fine innings.

*A tiny silver plaque
presented by the
Earl of Sheffield
to cricketer John Gilbert
for his impressive
scoring performance*

The Corporation and Guardians officials from Brighton had a day's excursion to Newick with a lunch at the Bull Inn followed by a cricket match between the two public bodies. Sports were held together with a dinner in the marquee.

About 100 people attended the Newick Independent United Friends Club anniversary at the Bull Inn. The band of the First Cinque Ports (Lewes) Rifles provided the music for dancing.

The employees from the smiths department at the Brighton railway works had an outing to Newick. Dinner was served in the marquee next to the Bull Inn followed by entertainment from the Works Brass Band and a piper in full Highland costume. The day finished with sports after the rain stopped with prizes including a silk handkerchief, shirt, box of cigars, trousers, hat and bottles of whiskey and brandy.

The Earl of Sheffield organised a cricket match at Sheffield Park between the Australian team and an eleven of England team. This was an extraordinarily popular event with as many as 26,000 spectators attending over the two days.

AUGUST 1884

The staff from The Pantechnican, Queens Road, Brighton had a day's outing in Newick with sports and dinner.

The Lady Vernons School and the Infant School had their annual treat at Newick Park courtesy of J H Sclater with a lunch, a visit to the gardens, presents, tea and singing.

The school children from the National School had their annual treat at Beechlands courtesy of Mr and Mrs Blaauw including racing, cricket, swinging, apple and money diving etc. The prizes for the athletic sports were toy locomotives, money boxes, monkey puzzles, carpenters tools, purses, combs, handkerchiefs, knives, balls etc. Books and prizes were also awarded for scripture examinations, good attendance, good conduct, home work and progress in study.

SEPTEMBER 1884

The house and bakehouse occupied by Mr Hemsley has been investigated by The Inspector of Nuisances because the privy and pig pounds are too close to the bakehouse and the drains to the cesspool are very defective. Action will have to be taken to remedy the health hazard.

The Cottagers Garden Show this year also had a loan exhibition of articles of historic interest – old needlework, firearms, silver, china, ornamental lamps, silks, coins, a man-trap etc. William Mullinger, the local stationmaster, supplied a display of telegraph instruments, burglar alarms, switches, electric motors, submarine cables, a working model steam engine and electric bells. Percy Gravely displayed some of his own oil paintings.

OCTOBER 1884

The new Newick Cricket Club had the end of season meeting at the Boys School with R Gravely as chairman. The balance sheet was presented together with the seasons results – only one win out of eight games. Mr Oldaker, the school headmaster, heads the batting average and J P Brook is the top bowler. Thanks were given to J H Sclater for allowing some of the matches to be played at Newick Park and thanks were also expressed to the officers of the old club for supplying materials. Disappointment was expressed at the club still not having a suitable home ground.

NOVEMBER 1884

Guy Fawkes night was celebrated again with vigour and enthusiasm. The procession comprised two fully dressed and mounted troopers, the commander-in-chief, the band, effigies of Guy and the Pope with followers in costume, torches and coloured lights. The 4-mile route was to Newick Lodge, Ketches, Newick Park, Reedens, The Rough and back to the Bull Inn. The event ended with the bonfire on The Green, fireworks and dancing.

NEWICK BOYS v. Mr T B POWELL'S XI

Played 1st October 1884

In this wind-up match at Newick on Wednesday the Boys made a highly creditable show against a strongish scratch side. Helped by the wicket the bowlers on both sides were very destructive, while the defensive batting of Osborn and T.Christmas deserves special mention.

Score:—

NEWICK BOYS

T.Christmas b. A.Tidy	0	c.Hodge b. Gravely	4
D.Tidy c. Oldaker b. A.Tidy	2	b. Brook	0
A.Richards b. A.Tidy	1	b. Brook	0
G.G.Wood c. Gravely b. A.Tidy	1	run out	4
A.Bates c. and b. A.Tidy	3	c. Fuller b. Gravely	2
K.Brooks b. Gravely	2	b. Brook	0
W.Wood run out	6	b. Brook	0
A.Osborn b. W.G.Powell	9	b. Brook	0
R.Dicker not out	1	b. Gravely	0
W.Page b. W.G.Powell	0	b. Brook	0
G.Dicker b. W.G.Powell	0	not out	3
Sundries	6	Sundries	3
	31		**18**

MR. POWELL'S ELEVEN.

W.G.Powell c.Page b. D.Tidy	1	not out	0
F.Gravely c. G.Wood b. D.Tidy	3	b. G.Wood	2
A.Tidy c. W.Wood b. D.Tidy	4		
J.Oldaker l.b.w. b. D.Tidy	0	not out	18
J.Brook b. G.Wood	2	c. G.Dicker b. D.Tidy	3
R.Fuller b. D.Tidy	6		
G.Hodge run out	1		
A.Cheale b. D.Tidy	1		
H.Farley b. G.Wood	0		
D.Christmas not out	2		
T.B.Powell b. D.Tidy	1	b. D.Tidy	0
Sundries	3	Sundries	4
	24		**27**

A cricket scorecard for the end of the season 1884. A few days after the match the scorecard was being used by Mr Oldaker in a handwriting exercise for the pupils at the National School

The Bonfire Boys had their annual supper at the Bull Inn courtesy of the new landlord Mr Neve, with toasts, songs, a handbell performance and finishing with a firework display.

The London Brighton and South Coast Railway Company intend to apply to the next session of Parliament for the stopping up of the public footpath which crosses the new railway line about 250 yards to the south-east of the station.

DECEMBER 1884

Mr Oldaker, the headmaster at the National School, is becoming increasingly concerned regarding the lack of assistance at the school.

JANUARY 1885

The Rev William Powell, the rector of Newick for the last 17 years, died, aged 68, from cancer in the stomach. He was a popular, genial gentleman and had a great interest in archaeology.

The new cricket club had a meeting at the Boys School to elect its officers. It was agreed to hire one of Mr Larkin's fields at Mitchelswood Farm for use as a practise and match ground.

FEBRUARY 1885

The Rev W Powell was interred in the family vault. Nearly all the tradesmen and leading residents of the village attended the funeral.

H A Day commenced duties as an assistant to Mr Oldaker at the National School.

MARCH 1885

The annual report of the Medical Officer of Health for the Chailey District was published in the newspaper.

The Rev Clement Powell was instituted by the Bishop of Chichester as the new rector for Newick following the death of the Rev W Powell.

APRIL 1885

Large numbers of army volunteers camped and billeted at Newick on their way to the huge review at Brighton.

A four-wheeled van travelling from Haywards Heath market to Little Horsted collapsed near Painters Farm when the front wheel came off. Thomas Wicks the driver employed by Mr Sturt at Little Horsted, was thrown out and badly injured his head on the stony ground. Mr Frank Gravely attended to his injuries at the Cottage Hospital.

An auction was held at the rectory on behalf of the executors of the late Rev William Powell with the sale of furniture, carpets, paintings, prints and other household goods, outdoor effects including 2 waggonettes, a 4-wheel phaeton, a donkey cart, harnesses, saddles etc together with livestock comprising 2 cows, a heifer and a pig and some meadow hay.

MAY 1885

Newick Cricket Club fixtures for this season have been determined. The new ground at Mitchelswood will afford the players better practise than they were able to get last year. The first game on the new ground was against Danehill. Newick won. Mr Neve from The Bull Inn provided the catering. A photograph of the team was taken: T Bates, J P Brook, H J Glover, H Gravely, A Hemsley, A Henty, S F Larkins, J Oldaker, F Potter, W F Rogers and A Tidy. K Walls was umpire and H D Chrismas scorer.

Newick cricket team May 1885

There was plenty of livestock for the annual fair on The Green with better business than usual. The pleasure fair was of the usual kind.

There were massive crowds of 5,000-6,000 to see the grand cricket match at Sheffield Park between Lord Sheffield's team, including W G Grace, and Alfred Shaw's Australian team. Refreshments and a band helped the event along and the beautiful gardens were to be admired.

JUNE 1885

The wives and children of the men employed on Mr Sclater's Newick Park estate were provided with tea and partook of an enjoyable evening courtesy of Mr Sclater.

A mad dog was running around the area and bit a little girl at Sutton Hall. The dog was captured by Mr Avery at Ricketts Farm Newick and destroyed.

Thomas B Fuller commenced teaching at the National School as a pupil-teacher on probation.

JULY 1885

The Independent United Friends Society had their annual business at the Bull Inn followed by a procession, a church service, dinner with the customary toasts and then some general amusements.

The employees of Reed and Son from Brighton had an outing to Newick by train and enjoyed themselves with cricket and other amusements. They were accompanied by Mr Page's band.

Mr Howell from Church Farm had a narrow escape from severe injury. A bull rushed at him and he fell heavily but luckily the bull was beaten off by Mr Howell's companions.

A diphtheria epidemic has spread in Newick in June and July affecting adults as well as children. Dr Gravely says preventative measures must be taken – disinfecting and isolation and, upon death, there should be early burial with the coffin filled with sawdust saturated in carbolic acid.

AUGUST 1885

Captain Henry Crichton Sclater has given worthy service in the Royal Artillery in the Soudan campaign, so the Queen has graciously approved his promotion to Major.

SEPTEMBER 1885

The boys of the National School had their annual treat, not at Beechland as usual, but at the Rectory courtesy of the Rev Clement Powell and Mrs Powell. The entertainment was cricket, bat and trap etc with prizes and tea.

Harvest Thanksgiving was held at the Zion Chapel.

A meeting was held in a marquee on The Green with the liberal candidate for the Mid or Lewes Division, W E Hubbard, speaking about his suggested thorough reform of land laws – doing away with transfer of land and enfranchisement of copyholders, that land should be held by a much larger number of owners and that there should be a future for the agricultural labourer with better tenure of land.

The Cottage Garden show was held at the National School Room with displays and exhibits of flowers, fruit and vegetables. The judges and those engaged in organising the show had dinner at The Crown Inn.

A Conservative Association meeting was held in the School Room in support of Sir Henry Fletcher, the parliamentary candidate for the Mid or Lewes Division.

The cricket club concluded its season with a married v single match and a dinner at the Bull Inn followed by toasts and songs.

OCTOBER 1885

A grand wedding was held for J H Sclater's third daughter, Jane Elizabeth Rachael Sclater, to Captain Robert Francis Gartside-Tipping from Ireland. The route between Newick Park and the church was decorated with arches of evergreens, flowers, flags and inscriptions. The honeymoon will be in Scotland and then the couple will go to India.

The girls from the Lady Vernon School together with infants from the Board School had a treat at Newick Park with sports, amusements, tea in the coach house and prizes for regular school attendance.

The Newick Cricket Club end of season meeting referred to the great benefits of the new Mitchelswood home ground hired on very reasonable terms. Steps have been taken to enlarge and improve the pitch. S F Larkins heads the batting average for the season with A Tidy topping the bowling.

The church choir had its annual supper at the Rectory with the Rev Clement Powell. Miss Kenward, the late organist, was presented with a handsomely bound volume of Hymns Ancient and Modern in recognition of her energetic services to the choir.

NOVEMBER 1885

A missionary meeting was held in the National School Room in support of the Society for the Propagation of the Gospel with the Rev E H Dodson speaking on the slave trade in Africa and his work in Zanzibar and Tristan da Cunha.

The Bonfire Boys had their annual supper at the Bull Inn with the brass band from Fletching providing entertainment.

DECEMBER 1885

A skilful and tasteful concert of bellringing was given to an appreciative audience in the National School Room by the Walford family comprising five brothers and sisters.

George Cottington from Jackeys Farm was killed when the traction engine he was driving from Newick to Sheffield Bridge toppled over an embankment. He was crushed by the weight of the thrashing machine which was being towed behind. His colleague Mr Salvage was injured and was taken to the Cottage Hospital.

The Sunday School boys and girls enjoyed a treat at the National School on New Year's Eve – tea, a magic lantern exhibition and gifts.

The Local Government Board Inspector, John Spear, visited Newick and recognises the need for improved drainage to the village.

JANUARY 1886

A meeting was held at the school room to pursue the idea of restoring and enlarging the church, an urgent necessity because of the very large congregations on Sundays. A committee was formed and work is hoped to start soon provided sufficient funds are found.

A lending library operates from the Rectory open every Monday 4 o'clock until 5 o'clock with a charge of 1 penny per month.

Henry Weston died aged 65.

The officers and boys of the Chailey industrial school under H J Glover provided an entertainment to a large audience at the National School with musical selections, scenes, readings, dialogue, etc.

The report of the Local Government Board Inspector has now been received following his visit to the District last month. The report is very critical stating that the administration of the Sanitary Authority is lax and that the Authority is failing to deal satisfactorily with nuisances.

FEBRUARY 1886

A dance was held at the National School with Mr Page's band which continued well into the morning. The proceeds go to the school.

William Fares, the fish hawker from Brighton, well known in the locality, died. He had arrived at the station with his heavy baskets of fish and, while walking to the village, near the Zion Chapel, collapsed and died.

A concert at the National School Room in aid of the church restoration fund raised £7.

MARCH 1886

The secretary of The Society for the Protection of Ancient Buildings has written to the Rev Clement Powell strongly urging that a new church should be built rather than extending the existing one or, if it is to be enlarged, then the extension should be on the north side.

The Newick Cricket Club had its annual meeting in the boys school to elect officers.

A meeting at the Lady Vernon school room has established a Newick branch of the South Saxon Habitation of the Primrose League. Members were enrolled and an executive committee organised.

The annual parish meeting at the Bull Inn re-appointed the officers of overseer, assistant overseer, surveyor of highways and assessors. This was followed by a dinner.

APRIL 1886

The Incorporated Society for Promoting the Enlargement, Building and Repairing of Churches and Chapels has voted £50 towards enlarging the church.

Her Majesty's Inspector made his annual examination of the school.

On Primrose Day, the first train of the day through Newick and Chailey station was decorated with primroses and ferns. The driver, stoker and guard also wore bunches of primroses.

Joseph Hammond the corn merchant and brewer lost his court case concerning payment for some beans.

MAY 1886

Restoring the church has commenced by Messrs Dobson and Son from Colchester to the plans of the architect John Oldrid Scott. The chancel is to be dismantled and re-erected a little further to the east and the nave enlarged. The north aisle will also be enlarged with a vestry on the end. Stone for the arcades will be gratuitously supplied from J H Sclater's quarries by Fount Hill. Heating apparatus will be installed, a new wooden block floor will be laid and new oak benches provided. The old pitch pine seats are being advertised for sale. Services will now have to be temporarily held in the National Boys school.

Thousands of spectators gathered at Sheffield Park where Lord Sheffield's XI, captained by W G Grace, played the Australians. No costs were spared in organising this lavish event in these lovely grounds.

The Newick Old Benefit Society held its annual event with the usual business, a parade with the Fletching Brass Band, dinner in the marquee next to the Bull Inn, amusements in the field and dancing. The Society had no church service this year because the church is being restored.

JUNE 1886

Mary Ponting was stabbed on Chailey Common. The assailant is still at large.

Dr Gravely still comments upon the inadequate drainage to the village. A sewer serves the houses between the Bull Inn and North Lodge but a sewer is needed to serve the other cottages to avoid the public nuisance of frequent emptying of cesspools.

The Zion Chapel held its 52nd anniversary.

The Barcombe Gospel Temperance Society held an open-air missionary meeting on The Green, bringing with them their drum and fife band.

62 year old John Hobbs, a carter at Colin Godman's Farm, Sheffield Forest, was found drowned in the river Ouse between Sheffield Park Station and Rotherfield Wood. The farmer, Daniel Watson, found the lifeless body gruesomely floating upright with the legs embedded in the sand and mud and the swollen and disfigured head just below the water level. PC Gower then examined the body.

A Girls Friendly Society has started in the village.

Henry Green, the 29 year old shoemaker, has been found guilty and given 6 months hard labour for stealing clothing from the house of George Avis.

A Newick cricket team 1886

JULY 1886

The Brighton Holy Trinity Church choir had an outing to Newick Park with boating on the lake, cricket, luncheon in the woods and tea courtesy of Mr Sclater.

The Independent United Friends Club held their annual dinner in a marquee at the Bull Inn followed by sports, cricket and dancing to the Fletching Brass Band.

The Newick branch of the Primrose League held a meeting at the Dowager Countess of Roden's house, North Lodge, with music, vocals, refreshments and a talk on politics and the conservative cause. The purpose of the league was explained in intending to break down the barriers between the classes and that all had a common interest at heart. In future the Newick Branch will be known as the 'Weald of Sussex Habitation'.

The auction of James Brook's Goldbridge Farm failed to reach the reserve price of £7000. The 187 acres includes the substantial farmhouse, arable, meadows, orchards, woodland, a pond, newly erected buildings and 4 acres of hops.

AUGUST 1886

Joseph Hammond has been given permission by the Bench to have an off-licence at his brewery premises.

(laughter).—The Bench, Mr Blencowe said, were in favour of the license by a majority, and it was therefore granted.

BEER LICENSE : NEWICK.

Mr Buckwell, of Brighton, applied on behalf of Mr Joseph Hammond, brewer, of Newick, for an off license for his premises at Newick. He explained that the applicant already held the brewer's license on the bottle and small cask trade, and therefore applied for the license to enable him to do so. The application was opposed by Mr M. S. Blaker, on behalf of Messrs Robbins and Sons, Messrs Norman, Messrs Beard, and Mr Alfred Hillman. He pointed out that there were already two full-licensed houses in Newick, the Bull and the Crown, and two beer houses, the Royal Oak and the Bricklayers Arms. There was also a place where it could be had in casks, and refreshments were sold at the station. Mr Buckwell, in reply to the Bench, said Mr Hammond would undertake not to carry on the jug trade if the license were given, and that being so the Bench granted the application.

Newspaper cutting on proposed off licence at brewery

The Weald of Sussex Habitation of the Primrose League held its fete at Newick Park with tea in the open air, walking around the attractive grounds, dinner, music, speeches and a political meeting.

The boys of the church choir boarded a special excursion train and visited the Indian and Colonial Exhibition in South Kensington, London.

The masons employed on rebuilding the church played a game of cricket against a team organised by Thomas Baden Powell at High Hurst.

Peter Rogers, the farm bailiff, was summoned at Lewes Petty Sessions for neglecting to have his child vaccinated. An order was made that he should comply.

Joseph Hammond (brewer)

JOSEPH HAMMOND

𝕭𝖗𝖊𝖜𝖊𝖗, 𝕸𝖆𝖑𝖙𝖘𝖙𝖊𝖗,

CORN, CAKE, SEED AND COAL

MERCHANT,

NEWICK, NEAR LEWES.

Agent for F. C. HILLS & Co.'s ARTIFICIAL MANURES.

Also Stores at Newick Station.

PRICES.

	36 Galls.		18 Galls.		9 Galls.
XXX ALE	54/-	...	27/-	...	13/6
XX ALE	45/-	...	22/6	...	11/3
X ALE	36/-	...	18/-	...	9/-
BA BITTER ALE	54/-	...	27/	...	13/6
BB ALE	36/-	...	18/-	...	9/-
B ALE	27/-	...	13/6	...	6/9
T TABLE ALE ...	18/-	...	9/-	...	4/6
SS STOUT	54/-	...	27/-	...	13/6
S STOUT	45/-	...	22/6	...	11/3
PORTER	36/-	...	18/-	...	9/-

Brewery price list 1886

A Newick brewery vessel

The Diocesan Inspector has praised the admirable tone in the National School. He states that Mr Oldaker's work is characterised by great kindness and earnestness and that the boys evidently appreciate the efforts the headmaster makes for them.

SEPTEMBER 1886

The annual cottagers show, held in the Rev Powell's Rectory grounds, was a great success. The marquee was illuminated in the evening when farmers, cottagers and tradespeople attended. J Pickett, the secretary, has been indefatigable in his work for these shows for 50 years. Prizewinners were A Bates, E and R Booker, E Brooks, I Collings, J Hills, G Homewood, T Mainwood, T Martin, D Martin, B Martin, W Martin, D Smith and J Wheatland.

John Gilbert was badly injured at the cricket match between Newick and Fletching played on the ground at Mitchelswood. He received a severe blow to the head from the ball. This pitch does tend to have a fiery character in dry weather.

H Weston is quitting Bretts Farm and is to sell by auction 5 draught horses some steers and his agricultural machinery including waggons, ploughs etc.

At the end of the cricket season S F Larkin headed the batting average with Gilbert Wood and A Osborne conspicuous for their bowling.

OCTOBER 1886

The girls from the Lady Vernon School and the infants from the Board School had their annual treat at Newick Park with sports, amusements, tea and presents for all.

A harvest home was held at Newick Park for Mr Sclater's employees with dinner, indoor amusements and songs. The weather was too wet for cricket.

The annual harvest thanksgiving service was held at the National School this year because the church is still being enlarged.

The Newick National School children had their annual treat at The Rectory courtesy of the Rev Clement Powell and Mrs Powell with tea, competitions, spelling, mental calculations, songs and prizes. Three cheers were given for the hosts followed by the National Anthem.

NOVEMBER 1886

A Choral Society has been formed for the parishes of Newick, Chailey and Fletching to achieve self improvement in music for its members, organisation of concerts in the three villages and performance of musical selections. The annual subscriptions will be 2s 6d and practice will be weekly.

The Gunpowder Plot celebrations this year started with torrents of rain while the Bonfire Boys were making their preparations. By 6 o'clock the weather improved and the procession commenced with mounted troopers, banners, guys, effigies and the Fletching Brass Band. The route was to the houses of the gentry, along The Rough which was a river of mud to the Bricklayers Arms for refreshments, then to Reedens and back to The Green. The spectacle included torches, coloured fire, Roman candles, tar barrels, sky rockets, the bonfire, burning of the effigies, dancing, fireworks and the National Anthem.

A pigeon shooting match was held in the field adjoining the old workhouse. W J Martin and W G Powell beat Mr Hammond and D H Neve 15 to 14 and also beat J P Brook and S F Larkin 5 points to 3. H Fuller, one of the helpers, escaped serious injury when one of the charges fell all about him with one shot piercing his nose and another striking him just below the eye. Competitors and their friends dined afterwards at the Bull Inn.

The Bonfire Boys had their annual supper at the Bull Inn with toasts, songs, the Fletching Brass Band and a firework display on The Green.

DECEMBER 1886

Amos Williams from Newick and Edward Heaseman from Barcombe were caught trespassing at Chailey. They made off leaving some nets, a small spade and a ferret. They were subsequently summoned. Amos was fined £1 and 11s costs. Edward did not appear at court.

Great gales swept southern England and the south coast with some deaths at sea.

Lord Sheffield has been most annoyed over the past autumn by a series of anonymous accusations regarding his grounds and has closed his cricket ground until the culprits are discovered and punished.

JANUARY 1887

The children of the Sunday School had a novel treat at the National School room. A classroom had been converted into a mock Post Office with Mr F Gravely officiating as postmaster and each child able to make an enquiry. This was followed by giving of presents, the National Anthem and each child taking home an orange, a cake and a bag of sweets.

A ball was held in the brewery courtesy of Mr Hammond with over 100 people attending and dancing till the morning hours. Mr Page provided music on the piano assisted by Mr Bates on violin, Mr Brooke on cornet and Mr Packham on piccolo. The proceeds went to the Cottage Hospital.

FEBRUARY 1887

The Newick Choral Union gave their first concert at the school room in Chailey with the Rev Clement Powell, Jessie Moore, Mabel Ingram, the Misses Blencowe, Mr Quirke and R H Powell providing a successful performance.

The adults of the Church choir had their annual supper at the Rectory courtesy of the Rev C Powell.

Mr Pollard, the church organist, is leaving Newick and was presented with a gold albert chain by the Rev Clement Powell.

The Lewes County Court settled a disputed account between George Wood the butcher and Absolom Hampton the blacksmith in favour of Mr Wood.

MARCH 1887

The Newick Cottage Hospital provided its sixteenth annual report showing that 21 patients have been treated over the year.

The annual hare hunt was held in Newick with the best chase being from Fount Hill to Home Farm and Goldbridge. This was followed by a dinner at the Bull Inn courtesy of the host Mr Neve.

The Cricket Club had its annual meeting presided over by Captain J R Sclater. Mr Sclater was thanked for the use on several occasions of his ground at Newick Park. T Baden Powell was thanked for use of his scoring tent.

The School Board members were re-elected – J H Sclater, Rev Clement Powell, F Bannister, H Howell and J Howell.

A Vestry meeting was held in the Bull Inn. J Isard and J Brook were elected as overseers for the parish with J Howell as the surveyor, John Picket as the assistant surveyor and collector of highway rates and W J Martin and W Freeland as the assessors. Also discussed was the requirement to enlarge the Lady Vernon girls school and the need to maintain the footpath between the National School and the church.

A meeting was held in the Rectory lecture room to discuss the nationwide appeal to establish an Imperial Institute as a celebration of the Queen's forthcoming Jubilee.

Four men had to restrain Mr Cottingham when he threatened to kill his mother. Dr Gravely considered he was mentally deranged so he ordered his removal to the asylum at Haywards Heath.

Lord Sheffield is becoming increasingly concerned regarding anonymous letters being sent to him, one referring to adultery and whoremongery in Sheffield Park. Another says everybody is laughing at the Lord and that he should get out and about to see how his cottages and farms have fallen down.

APRIL 1887

The Women's Jubilee Offering Fund has raised £7 17s 6d from 300 contributors in the Parish.

A well attended meeting was held at the National School Room for the parishioners to discuss how to celebrate the forthcoming Queen Victoria's Jubilee commemorating her 50 years on the throne. Mr Gravely curiously objected to his name being used in regard to the notice of the meeting. John Howell, the churchwarden, responded to his objection at which point there were murmurs and whisperings amongst the audience, including 'punch his head' and 'go into him John'! The meeting then began to disperse, so the steps to celebrate the Jubilee will be taken under other auspices.

The annual fair was held on the Green with cattle, horses and one pen of sheep. Prices were low and much remained unsold. Entertainments kept the event alive with swings, roundabouts, shooting galleries and coconut alleys. Following local disquiet public notices were erected on behalf of the Lord of the Manor to require the parties to leave The Green by daybreak the following morning. An attempt may be made to put an end to the custom.

NEWICK.

THE FAIR.—This annual event took place on Saturday. Prices were low, but fluctuated considerably. Some good two-yearlings were on view, the highest price reached being £13. 10s., obtained for Mr. Coteoworth by some capital beasts, and the lowest price for beasts of the same class was as low as £5. Yearlings fetched from £3 to £7, and one lot of runts £13 apiece, barrens £6 to £12, milch cows and calf £7 to £14. There were no pigs on sale, and the one solitary pen of sheep, belonging to Mr. Hart, of Lindfield, was unsold, and sent off to Chailey market after the fair closed. Among the horses on view was a splendid colt belonging to Mr. Head, of Goldstrow Farm. It was greatly admired, but it did not find a buyer. The quality of the majority of the other horses was poor. The proprietors of swings, roundabouts, shooting galleries, cocoa-nut alleys, &c., were well patronised. According to public notices displayed in the village, issued by order of the lord of the manor, the parties all took their departure by daybreak on Sunday morning. Numerous complaints are made by the inhabitants concerning the stay of such an objectionable class of people so near to the permanent dwellings, and it is probable that an attempt will be made to put a stop to the custom.

Newspaper cutting on the village fair – 1887

The Reverend J Fairclough gave a talk at the National School Room, on behalf of the Society for the Propagation of the Gospel, on his 20 years of missionary work in Burma.

MAY 1887

A general meeting of Newick residents agreed to observe 21st June as a general holiday to celebrate the Queen's Jubilee. A committee has been appointed to decide the form of the festivities. James Brook has agreed to make available a recreation meadow at the rear of the brewery.

The letter box at the railway station is now emptied twice daily.

The Newick Old Benefit Society held its annual event with business at the Bull Inn and a procession with the Fletching Brass Band. There was no church service this year as the church is still being restored. A meal was provided by Mr Standen, the new host at the Bull Inn. This was followed by sports.

Prizes of books, atlases, drawing materials, satchels etc were awarded to the children of the National School for good attendance and for the annual examinations.

John Funnell died aged 74. He had been a schoolmaster at Newick and Chailey, was a respected land surveyor, a self-taught landscape painter and author of a volume of poems and verse entitled 'Poetical Dialogues Between Fancy and Reason' (1860). The villages' other famous authors were the late James Taylor who published 'The Sussex Garland' 26 years ago in January 1851 and W H Blaauw who wrote 'The Barons War' (1844). John Funnel's son William, who has assisted his father as a land surveyor, will now continue the business.

JUNE 1887

The village had an outbreak of scarlet fever. The first sign was in a cottage where some needlework had been brought from an infected cottage in Newhaven.

The Victoria Jubilee commenced with church bells ringing at 6 o'clock in the morning. The village was cheerfully decorated with flags, banners and bunting. A service was held in the School Room. 600 men and boys sat down to dinner in a marquee and 700 women and children for tea. 960 pounds of roast and boiled beef was eaten, 640 pounds of plum pudding and 108 gallons of ale, with the surplus distributed to the poor of the Parish. There were Punch and Judy shows, roundabouts, the Fletching Brass Band, coconut alleys, egg races, blindfold wheelbarrow races and other sports. James Anderson caused great amusement climbing the 35 foot high greasy pole. A donkey race was intended but not enough donkeys could be found in the Parish. All the children were given a Jubilee mug. The evening was taken up with dancing and music, rockets, fireworks and a bonfire. The day finished with the National Anthem. A day ever to be remembered.

There is discussion on whether a pump with a well should be provided on The Green to celebrate the Jubilee.

The London Brighton and South Coast Railway Company has responded to a petition by agreeing to add an extra train in the evenings.

JULY 1887

Samuel Standen, the landlord at the Bull Inn, was fined £6 9s 6d, including costs, for allowing gambling on his premises.

About 250 people from the Weslyan Sunday School from Brighton had a day out at Newick Park courtesy of J H Sclater.

The Independent United Friends Club held their annual dinner at the Bull Inn but there was no procession or service this year because the church is still being restored and is unavailable for use. Sports were held and the Fletching Brass Band played.

The church was finally re-opened after the extensive restoration and extension started in May last year and was consecrated by the Lord Bishop at a bright and joyful ceremony. The church can now accommodate nearly 400.

The Newick Choral Union, formed last November, has held some very successful concerts although the financial statement for the season shows a deficit of £2 8s 6d.

AUGUST 1887

The boys from the National School had their annual treat at Beechland, courtesy of Mr and Mrs Blaauw with tea, sports and amusements including three-legged races, obstacle race, sack race, apple bobbing, a jingling match, swinging, see-saw and cricket. The employees of the estate also joined in the fun. One poor lad had his fingers pinched under the see-saw plank. Dr Gravely attended and suggested that the boy was lucky not to have lost both fingers.

The choir boys together with some adult members had a treat with a trip to the American Exhibition in London including the spectacular Buffalo Bill Wild West Show.

The debt for the church restoration is now down to £400. A new altar cloth has been presented, a new cover proposed for the font and a coloured glass window presented by Arthur Powell.

J Oldaker arranged a cricket match between the Newick 1st XI and a team of 27 others! This created a great interest from the spectators especially when the team of 27 were fielding – like a swarm of bees on the pitch.

130 children from the infants board school under their mistress Miss Bayliss and from the Lady Vernon School for girls under Miss Warner had their annual treat at Newick Park with games, tea and presents for each child.

SEPTEMBER 1887

The annual harvest festival at the church displayed an immense supply of flowers, fruit and vegetables. The festival created particular interest this year now that the church has been enlarged.

A harvest home was held for the men and lads engaged on the Newick Park estate courtesy of Mr Sclater, with a roast dinner and plum pudding, toasts, cricket between the marrieds and the singles with music in the evening.

OCTOBER 1887

John Howell is selling the stock of Church Farm including six draught horses, a cob, heifers, a bull together with farming implements, a waggon, a 4-wheel chaise etc.

A football club has now been formed for Newick. The president is the Rev Clement Powell with J Oldaker as captain and T Chrismas as vice-captain/treasurer/secretary. The managing committee is T Freeland, G Gibson, A Hemsley, G Wood, G H Chrismas and G Staplehurst.

fee and to admit the scholars without any charge for the instruction given. In addition to the elementary subjects, the syllabus of instruction includes drawing and geography.

FOOTBALL CLUB.—A meeting was held in the National School-room on Wednesday evening for the purpose of forming a football club in Newick. The game was started here last winter and as it then met with considerable favour it was resolved to try to organise a club this season. The Rev. C. Powell presided at the meeting and there was a very fair attendance. Mr. Oldaker proposed that a club be formed for the encouragement of football under the Association Rules, which was seconded by Mr. G. H. Chrismas and carried unanimously. The next business was the consideration of rules for the club and a list, drafted by Mr. Oldaker, was submitted to the meeting and after some discussion and amendment they were adopted as the club rules. Officers were then proposed as follows :—President, Rev. C. Powell ; Vice-Presidents, Mr. T. St. L. Blaauw, Mr. R. Gravely, Captain G. R. Keene, Mr. T. B. Powell, Mr. W. F. Rogers, Captain J. R. Sclater; captain of the eleven, Mr. J. Oldaker ; vice-captain, Mr. T. Chrismas ; treasurer and secretary, Mr. T. Chrismas ; committee, Messrs. G. H. Chrismas, T. Freeland, G. Gibson, A. Hemsley, G. Staplehurst, Gilbert Wood. It was announced that matches were in course of arrangement with clubs and schools of moderate strength and it was left to the committee to complete the season's programme, to decide upon the selection of the club colours and to carry out other necessary details. A vote of thanks to the chairman brought the meeting to a close.

Newspaper cutting on proposed football club – October 1887

Evening classes in elementary subjects, geography, drawing etc are being held again this year at the National School with fees now abolished.

30-40 working men from Fletching have received an intimation that they may lose their jobs at Sheffield Park if the writers of the anonymous letters to the Earl of Sheffield are not brought to light. They caused a commotion in the village when they assembled at the

Bull Inn to persuade the landlord, Mr Standen, to disclose the names of the perpetrators. Mr Standen was unable to assist.

Newick Cricket Club had its annual dinner at the Bull Inn. The club is now looked upon as a permanent institution in the village.

Mr Cottingham was seen in Newick and had to be escorted back to the asylum at Haywards Heath.

NOVEMBER 1887

Samuel Standen, the landlord at the Bull Inn, was convicted of harbouring a constable when on duty and was ordered to pay a penalty of £1 and 12 shillings costs.

The gunpowder plot celebrations were held with the Fletching Brass Band, a brilliantly lit procession, marchers in costumes ranging from a Franciscan friar to a common cornsack, banners proclaiming 'Success to the Newick Bonfire Boys' and 'Long Live Our Supporters', flags, tar barrels, effigies of Guy and the Pope all completed with a bonfire, dancing, Rule Britannia and God Save The Queen. There was greater variety and more originality than previous years.

The Bonfire Society supper was held at the Bull Inn with the secretary G H Chrismas presiding. Following the meal, songs and toasts, there were fireworks on The Green.

The annual tithe audit was held with a dinner at The Crown Inn for the principal tithe payers. A petition had been submitted to abate the tithes this year because of the badly depressed state of agriculture. Although the Rev C Powell had sympathy he felt it was inappropriate for the payments to be waived.

DECEMBER 1887

A successful subscription dance was held at the National School with about 120 participants. Dancing continued until 5 o'clock in the morning.

JANUARY 1888

The labourer Alfred Hodges from Newick stole some spectacles and haberdashery from a hawker, Anne Chaplin, at the Bull Inn in December. He has been found guilty and sentenced to a month of hard labour.

The Sunday School children had their annual treat with tea and entertainment from a conjurer and ventriloquist from London. The deserving children received gifts of books.

George Henry Gilham took over as stationmaster from William Mullinger. Mr Mullinger who has been at the station since its opening was an obliging and tactful gentleman.

The girls school and the infants school were closed for a time because of an outbreak of scarlet fever. Four houses have been disinfected. Dr Gravely is concerned regarding the apathy and indifference of parents reporting this infection at the early stages which results in spread of the disease.

The concert at the National School, organised by Mrs Rogers, was crowded.

A meeting of the Church Restoration Committee at the Rectory noted that a deficit of £352 18s 9d remains.

FEBRUARY 1888

A Conservative meeting was held at the National Schoolroom with the object of forming a local branch of the Mid Sussex Conservative Association.

The Railway Company laid on a late train to Newick and Chailey station for those returning from the Dick Whittington pantomime in Brighton.

The adult members of the church choir had their annual supper at the Rectory classroom.

The annual report of the Chailey Union Rural Sanitary Authority refers to the continuing need for a suitable drainage system for the village. Mr Sclater has now granted permission for a sewer to be laid through a field on Bretts Farm.

Some haystacks just to the north east of the church on Mrs Archer's farm caught alight at about 11 o'clock in the evening. The Parish constable called Mark Wood to assist and the Lewes fire brigade attended. Water had to be pumped from a stream until it ran dry and then from a pond, once the ice was broken. One stack was completely destroyed but six tons were saved from the other. The wheelwright G H Chrismas was injured during the event when a helper pushed a prong through his foot while trying to remove the hay.

MARCH 1888

William Mullinger, the former stationmaster at Newick and Chailey station, was presented with a purse of £20, a silver teapot and an illuminated address, on behalf of Newick and Chailey residents in recognition of his able and efficient service at the station.

The Newick lending library will now be for adults as well as children.

A confirmation service was held at the church for 97 participants from Newick and the surroundings.

The annual Vestry meeting at the Bull Inn, presided over by Rev C Powell, received the church accounts as satisfactory. R Gravely is appointed as churchwarden as before with J P Brook and A Tidy as overseers, F Bannister as peoples warden and A Hampton and G Dicker as sidesmen. Mr Howell will continue as surveyor, John Pickett assistant overseer with W Freeland and W J Martin as assessors.

APRIL 1888

Mary Anne Archer died aged 85 and was buried in the family vault.

Business was not as brisk as last year at the annual Spring livestock fair on The Green. This was particularly because the date clashed with the regularly held livestock market at Chailey. There was the usual attraction of the pleasure fair.

The church font now has a new cover of solid oak with ornamental ironwork.

The cover to the church font

MAY 1888

The Newick Cricket Club annual meeting recognised the excellent work on the upkeep of the Mitchelswood home ground with the helpful use of a heavy roller from J H Sclater. Mr Sclater was also thanked for use of his ground at Newick Park and T B Powell was thanked for use of his scoring tent.

Drainage has been completed in the south western part of the village which will enable cesspools here to be abolished.

The Cottage Hospital presented its annual report showing that 21 cases had been dealt with over the year.

The church restoration fund now has the debt diminished to only £180. The old church seats raised a good sum.

The recently formed Newick Football Club held its first annual meeting. Mr T Chrismas, the secretary, reported a balance of 14s 6d.

Mr W J Martin and Mr G Starr were thanked for the kind use of their fields for matches and practise.

A concert on behalf of the Newick Cricket Club was held at the Boys School with songs and music. £6 was raised for the funds.

The Parish lending library is continuing to flourish.

There have been good examination results in the schools.

JUNE 1888

James Brook of Goldbridge is complaining that water on his land is being polluted by sewage discharge.

The quarterly meeting of the clergy of the Rural Deanery of Pevensey III was held at Newick in the Rectory.

JULY 1888

30 employees of Messrs Bostel Bros of Brighton had an outing to Newick with a dinner at the Bull Inn courtesy of the host Mr Starr, cricket, songs, music, walks by the river, drives into the countryside and visits to the strawberry gardens and cherry orchards. Prizes were awarded for three-legged races, leap-frog races etc.

The Independent United Friends Club had its annual fete with a procession with the Fletching Brass Band attending, a church service, lunch in a marquee at the Bull Inn courtesy of the host Mr Starr, together with outdoor amusements and dancing.

About 40 employees from the upholstery department of Hanningtons and Sons from Brighton had their outing to Newick. Dinner was served in a marquee at the Bull Inn. The entertainment was cricket, country walks, songs, sports and trap excursions into the countryside. Messrs Davis from Brighton took photographs.

Members of the Recreation Club of The Greyhound in Brighton came to Newick in horse brakes and a waggonette for an annual treat. They dined at the Bull Inn and held sports.

The members of the choir had a trip to Crystal Palace seeing the gardens and enjoying rides on the switchback railway and the toboggan slide.

A large number of employees of Messrs Lynn and Sons, builders from Brighton, had an excursion to Newick in 16 cabs. They engaged in cricket, quoits and sports with lunch in a marquee at the Bull Inn followed by more sports and some rambles around the village.

On the anniversary of the re-opening of the church after its restoration, the outstanding debt has now been cleared.

The choir of the Holy Trinity Church in Brighton arrived in Newick in 2, four-horse coaches for lunch at The Crown Inn. This was followed by a trip to Newick Park to be shown the gardens by the head gardener Mr Potter and then cricket, stoolball, racing and boating on the lake. After tea at The Crown Inn the party returned to Brighton.

AUGUST 1888

Robins and Son, brewers from Brighton, had a summer outing to Newick in two four-in-hands with lunch at the Bull Inn, cricket, quoits, sports and tea.

The girls from the Lady Vernon school and the infants from the Board School had a treat at Newick Park with racing, swinging, stoolball, tea on the lawn and presents.

The boys from the National School, under the charge of the headmaster Mr Oldaker, went to Beechlands for their annual treat. The party enjoyed swings, see-saws, apple-bobbing, races and a fine tea. As usual the estate employees were given a day off work and joined in with the sports including a tug-of-war between the marrieds and the singles.

SEPTEMBER 1888

The employees of Messrs Balchin and Son, the floricultural nurseries at Hassocks, had an outing to Newick. After lunch in the Bull Inn and a game of cricket the party had dinner with the customary toasts and then songs and music. After some short drives and strolls in the countryside the visitors travelled back home.

The annual Cottagers Garden Show was held in the National School Room with some fine displays of vegetables, fruit and flowers. The judges and officials had lunch at the Crown Inn.

A few children were absent from school because of whooping cough. Others are temporarily employed in the harvest fields and hop gardens.

The Weald of Sussex Habitation of the Primrose League, covering Newick, Chailey, Barcombe and Hamsey, visited Newick Park, arriving in waggonettes, brakes and other conveyances. The party walked in the fine gardens, played crickets, quoits, stoolball and other games and were entertained by the Lewes Town Band under Mr Gates. This was followed by tea, toasts and thanks and a talk on political topics. A clasp was awarded to Alfred Hemsley for his special services over the year, particularly for finding new members.

OCTOBER 1888

At the annual meeting of the Newick Football Club officers were appointed with J Oldaker presiding.

The Bonfire Society held their annual meeting at the Bull Inn with H Chrismas presiding.

The Newick Choral Union, having been somewhat inactive for a season, is now re-formed with appointment of officers and weekly practices.

Prizes were awarded to the successful exhibitors at last month's Cottagers Garden Show.

The Newick Park harvest home was held for the estate employees with cricket followed by supper chaired by the farm bailiff T Richards.

The annual Cricket Club supper was held at the Bull Inn.

Richard Fuller known as 'Crump' Fuller, a painter, plumber and glazier for many years and much respected, died aged 73 years. The Fuller business was started nearly 100 years ago in 1792.

Richard Fuller
(1815-1888)

NOVEMBER 1888

The Earl of Sheffield is receiving more anonymous letters, this time with a threat of murder by Jack the Ripper. The name is no doubt a hoax but the letters are taken as offensive, referring to tenants being turned out of their homes. A reward of £250 is being offered for information on the perpetrator.

Guy Fawkes night was celebrated in the usual manner with a procession marching via the Rectory, Reedens, Western Road etc with the Cooksbridge Fife and Drum Band, guys, tar barrels and banners proclaiming 'Success to the Bonfire Boys', 'Long Live Our Supporters', 'Cheer Boys Cheer', and 'No Popery'. The bonfire was sodden but it did burn with the scene brightened by Chinese lanterns around The Green.

The late John Weston's carpentry effects were sold from his residence on The Green, including his tools, benches, grindstone, timber, ladders, wattles, hand truck, chests and household furniture.

The annual rent audit for Newick Park and the Beechlands Estate was held at The Crown Inn followed by dinner for the tenants.

The members of the Bonfire Society had their annual supper at the Bull Inn including toasts and songs followed by a firework display.

Evening classes have commenced again at the National School at 3 pence per week for reading, writing and arithmetic.

DECEMBER 1888

The perpetrator of the threats of murder against the Earl of Sheffield has been before the winter assizes. Edward Grover has been found not guilty and discharged. Although having made the threats in a half drunken state it was without serious intention to carry out the threat.

A window in the south side of the chancel now has new coloured glass in memory of the late Mrs Archer of Newick Lodge. It depicts Isiah, David and Moses.

JANUARY 1889

The boys and girls from the Sunday School had their annual treat in the National School Room with tea and crackers. Prizes were awarded to the most meritorious scholars. What appeared to be a huge snowball was rolled in out of which Father Christmas appeared giving gifts for all. The party goers went home with the traditional cake and orange.

The church choir had a treat at the Rectory Classroom courtesy of the Rev C Powell and Mrs Powell with tea, songs and a novel theatrical performance entitled 'Bennibel' or 'Victim of Vanity'.

The Newick Choral Union gave a concert of songs and music to a packed school room.

Special late trains run on Mondays to Newick and Chailey station for those getting home from the pantomime in Brighton.

FEBRUARY 1889

The Newick branch of the Primrose League held a well attended lecture at the School Room. W P Banks of the National Union spoke on the Irish question using a magic lantern with dissolving views.

MARCH 1889

A supper was provided at the National School for about 30 pupils attending evening classes. R Gravely brought along a mechanical model which demonstrated the force of rotating motion.

There is now a Parish Nurse in residence – Nurse Kenton.

The annual Parish meeting was held at the Bull Inn with appointment of some of the officers followed by a dinner.

The local branch of the Mid-Sussex Conservative Association had their annual meeting at the National School presided over by Captain J R Sclater.

The eighteenth annual report of the Cottage Hospital shows that 23 patients were treated over the year.

APRIL 1889

The election of the Parish's surveyor of highways caused some excitement. Handbills were posted all over the village for the candidates – John Howell the retired farmer and Joseph Hammond the brewer. Despite some concern that Mr Howell now lives in Brighton, somewhat detached from the village, he was voted in, showing that there is still good feeling towards him. Nevertheless a little disturbance followed the declaration when he was struck on the head by a brick-bat.

A party was held at Beechlands by Mr and Mrs Blaauw to bid farewell to Miss Mitchell who has given 9 years service there. She is now getting married.

Joseph Hammond, the brewer, provided a farewell gathering for his son A Hammond and niece who are going to America. The large brewery room was suitably decorated and dancing continued until daylight.

If farmers in the district can supply 400 gallons of milk daily by mid-summer Lord Sheffield will provide a milk separator at Sheffield Park by Michaelmas so that all available milk in the neighbourhood could be utilised and a market found.

MAY 1889

The fourth concert of Newick Choral Society was held at the National School Room with a fair attendance despite the bad weather.

A handsome lectern, designed by J O Scott and made by the builder W J Martin, has been placed in the church together with a new bible presented by T St Leger Blaauw from Beechlands.

Thomas and Lucy Henty, both in their 70's from Founthill, held their golden wedding anniversary. They had 14 children.

The evening classes at the National School are currently well attended.

The Old Benefit Society held its annual festival with a church service, a parade through the village with the Fletching Brass Band followed by dinner in a marquee at the Bull Inn and then dancing.

Newick gardeners are being driven to desperation to control an epidemic of slugs. Hundreds of bushels of lime are being used to keep their numbers down and at Newick Park they are even using a night watchman to kill them by the knife.

JUNE 1889

The cricket club produced its 5th annual report showing that the club is flourishing.

JULY 1889

The Independent United Friends Club held their ninth anniversary with a procession, a church service, amusements and a dinner at the Bull Inn. The Fletching Brass Band provided music and dancing enlivened the evening.

Lewes Petty Sessions fined Charles Carvill, from Mitchelswood, five shillings for failing to have a licence for his dog.

Newick church choir had a thoroughly enjoyable outing by train to the London Zoological Gardens, the Moore and Burgess Minstrels in St James Hall and a meal in St James Hall in Piccadilly.

New stained glass is provided in the church window on the south side of the chancel in memory of the late Hon Charles Cornwallis Chetwynd.

Volunteer soldiers gathered at Sheffield Park for a march past review and a mock battle with guns blazing together with races, tug-of-war and sports.

An auction is to be held. Lot 1 is a block of cottages in 3 tenements abutting The Green. Lot 2 is an adjacent 2 bedroom dwelling facing The Green with piggery and the shoemakers shop occupied by Lewis Arthur Towner.

AUGUST 1889

Jacob Roberts Hoste, a tramp, has been remanded to do ten days hard labour for stealing a bag of corn samples from Mr Hammond, the corn merchant from Newick.

The children of the Lady Vernon School had their annual treat at Newick Park with games, tea, a stoolball match, presents for all and prizes to two scholars for good conduct. The mistress Miss Warner is leaving the school to be married and was presented with a Queen Anne tea pot and a cream jug. The day finished with the National Anthem.

Lady Vernon School children

A successful Cottage Garden Show was held at the National School.

The Crown Inn Benefit Society, now 30 years old, has declined to less than a dozen members so it is to be amalgamated with the Newick Old Benefit Society. The annual supper, with speeches and toasts, was the last.

James Miles, the publican at The Crown Inn for the last seven years, has been fined £2 with 10 shillings costs at the Lewes Petty Sessions for allowing the public house to remain open during prohibited hours.

SEPTEMBER 1889

J Oldaker, the headmaster at the National School, married Helena Rosa Warner, the headmistress at the Lady Vernon School. The past and present scholars of the school gave him a polished oak writing cabinet.

The Newick Football Club annual meeting at the National School elected its officers. Concern was expressed at the lack of clubs in the immediate neighbourhood necessitating travelling further afield to find opponents.

A scarlet fever outbreak closed the schools for a while during August and September. Children doing the hop picking also caused low attendance at the school.

The Newick Park harvest home was held for the employees of the estate with dinner, toasts and a game of cricket between the marrieds and the singles. The hay harvest this year was the finest ever known.

OCTOBER 1889

The cricket club had their annual dinner at the Bull Inn.

The annual harvest thanksgiving service raised £14 3s 3½d to be divided between the Church Missionary Society and Newick Cottage Hospital.

A memorial window and brass plate was provided in the church to the late Mrs Archer from Newick Lodge who died last year aged 85.

The managers of the National School presented the headmaster, John Oldaker, with a silver sugar basin and tongs in celebration of his marriage last month and for his last 8 years of service.

Whilst cleaning windows at Newick Park Alfred Marchant, employed by E H and R Fuller, fell from his ladder and badly injured his hip. He was attended by Mr Gravely and was taken to the Cottage Hospital.

A Mr Andrews, on his way back to his Cockfield Lane lodgings after working at The Rectory, stumbled and was badly injured with his bone protruding through the flesh. He was found by Fred Booker and was taken home and then to the Cottage Hospital. The next day he was sent to the County Hospital.

NOVEMBER 1889

The Guy Fawkes celebrations were much larger than usual this year with the added benefit of some fine weather. The procession included banners, guys, the Pope effigy, masqueraders, torches, the Chailey Drum and Fife Band, two mounted troopers together with a jockey on the pony Lazurus, one of the popular village pets, creating much amusement. The route followed from the Bull Inn to Newick Park, Colonels Bank, Reedens, visiting the gentry on the way and then back to The Green. A fine bonfire was lit in front of the Bull Inn with a firework display of rockets, wheels, squibs, crackers, Newick rousers and firing of a powerful charge of gunpowder from the blacksmiths anvil.

The Black Pearl Minstrels from Haywards Heath gave an entertainment of comic and sentimental songs at the National School in aid of the cricket club.

Some of the tenants of J H Sclater and T St Leger Blaauw dined at the Bull Inn following the rent audit.

The Bonfire Boys had their annual supper at the Bull Inn followed by a firework display.

Newick beat Chailey at whist at Mr Bannister's.

The Rev J H Collom gave a talk at the National School on his 32 years of missionary work in Canada.

DECEMBER 1889

The Rev J Parker from Groombridge gave some lectures with lantern slides on the history of the Church of England.

A presentation was made at the Rectory by the Rev C Powell to Mrs Reilly who has played the harmonium in the church for the last 3 years. The gift given was an American organ. Mrs Fuller who has also played the harmonium on several occasions was given a marble timepiece.

100 people attended the annual ball in the National School with dancing to W Page's band from Lewes until 5 o'clock in the morning. Philip Turner did the catering as usual.

There was a large attendance at the special morning service on St Thomas's day to see and hear the newly installed church organ with its 970 pipes built by the Casson Positive Organ Co. Mr Luard Selby from Pimlico gave an organ recital.

The church organ

JANUARY 1890

The Sunday School children had their annual treat at the National School with tea, prizes, football, a ventriloquist and conjurer from London and finishing with the National Anthem, presents and a cake and orange for everybody.

A concert raised money for the organ fund – songs, music, humour and readings from 'Three Men in a Boat'.

An influenza epidemic, colds and bronchial problems in the village resulted in temporary closure of the girls and infants schools and a difficulty in raising a football team.

A concert in the National School Room had a large audience and raised funds for the Cottage Hospital.

The funeral was held of George Wood, the well known and respected tradesman, who died at the age of 50 from inflammation of the lungs. Nearly all the tradesmen of Newick attended.

FEBRUARY 1890

The Parish Nurse, Nurse Kenton, will need more support if her good work is to continue.

81 year old Thomas Kingsland, who had been the gardener at High Hurst for 44 years, died in tragic circumstances. After standing with his back to an open fire he fell and was found with the seat of his trousers burning. When R Gravely attended to him he was in a half conscious state and badly burned, including his hands. He died from shock.

Mr and Mrs Freeland from the grocers and drapers shop on The Green had their silver wedding anniversary. They received silver salt cellars in a Morocco case from their sons and daughters.

The church choir boys had a treat in the Rectory Classroom with tea, games and refreshments.

J G Buckmaster, from the Science and Art department at South Kensington, gave a lecture in the National School on farming. 50 or more people attended.

MARCH 1890

Ann Doust's tenant at Rose Cottage was fined at the County Court for chopping down a cherry tree in the front of the cottage.

The Newick school board now comprises Rev C Powell, F Bannister, H Howell and Captain J R Sclater. J Howell who now lives in Brighton did not seek re-election.

The Ladytide Vestry meeting agreed a voluntary church rate of 2d in the pound to pay off the balance of £27 due on account of expenses for preparing the additional piece of land to the churchyard back in 1863. Overseers and the highway surveyor were appointed as well as 2 assessors.

APRIL 1890

The Newick Cricket Club held its annual meeting in the National School with election of officers.

A cream and butter factory has now been provided near Sheffield Park Station.

The National School children had a half-day holiday because of the Newick fair.

MAY 1990

70 children attending the Gospel Mission services were given tea and then enjoyed sports for prizes.

The Newick Football Club had their annual meeting at the National School.

The Lewes Cyclists Club had an evening trip to Newick.

Lord Sheffield's cricket team again entertained the Australians at Sheffield Park.

Mr B Luard Selby gave a recital of music on the new church organ which is now finally completed. The recital in December was done under great difficulties because the instrument was unfinished.

The Newick Old Benefit Society held its annual meeting with a service, a procession with the Fletching Brass Band and a dinner in the marquee at the rear of the Bull Inn courtesy of the new landlord Mr Avery. This was followed by outdoor amusements.

JUNE 1890

A Lewes and District Working Men's Liberal Association meeting was held on Newick Green in heavy rain. Mr H Pumphrey and Rev C D Badland speaking from a wagon in front of the Bull Inn condemned the government and all its works.

The government's school inspector speaks favourably of discipline and teaching at the National School.

JULY 1890

The Independent United Friends Club had their annual dinner at the Bull Inn. John Pickett, who has not missed a feast for over 40 years, was regrettably unable to attend because of illness. The Fletching Brass Band provided the music.

John Tidy (1827-1890)

Volunteer soldiers arrived at Newick and Chailey station and headed north to engage in mock battles at Sheffield Park followed by a review.

John Tidy, the corn dealer at Newick for many years, died at the age of 63. He was a well respected and genial gentleman with a humorous temperament. For the last 14 years he has been the assistant overseer at Fletching. He was a prominent member of the church choir with a deep and powerful bass voice.

AUGUST 1890

The pupils of the Lady Vernons School had their treat in Newick Park with games, races, tea on the lawn, prizes and presents for good attendance and progress.

The boys from the National School had their annual treat at Beechland in glorious weather with races, sports, prizes and tea under the shade of the beautiful limes. The day finished with the National Anthem, three cheers for Mrs Blaauw and buns and cakes being distributed.

SEPTEMBER 1890

The Newick Cottagers Garden Show was held, not at the National School as usual, but at the Rectory, attracting a large number of visitors to see the exhibits in the marquee. The Chailey Industrial School Band, under the direction of Mr Glover, provided musical entertainment. The weather was fine all day long.

The Bonfire Society held its meeting to elect the chairman W Freeland, the secretary G H Chrismas and decided fees for members etc.

Members of the church choir had an outing to Chichester Cathedral.

A meeting was held on The Green with the Lewes branch of the Protestant Alliance preaching on 'The Errors of Romanism' urging people to practise the teaching of the Bible and to instruct their children to do the same.

The cricket club had their annual supper at the Bull Inn with a summary of the season, toasts and songs.

OCTOBER 1890

Prizes were awarded in the Rectory Classroom for last month's Cottagers Garden Show.

The Newick Park harvest home was held for the farm workmen, gardeners and others employed by Mr Sclater with dinner, obligatory toasts and cricket.

NEWICK is a parish and pretty village, 4½ miles west from Uckfield, 8 north from Lewes, in the Mid division of the county, Barcombe hundred, Lewes rape, petty sessional division and county court district, Chailey union, rural deanery of Pevensey (third division), archdeaconry of Lewes and diocese of Chichester. The London, Brighton and South Coast Railway Company have a line from Lewes to East Grinstead, with a station in Chailey parish adjoining. The river Ouse flows through the parish. The church of St. Mary is an ancient edifice of stone, in the Norman and later styles, and consists of chancel, nave of four bays, north aisle and a low embattled western tower containing a clock and 6 bells : in 1887 the church was thoroughly restored and enlarged, the chancel being rebuilt further east and the nave and aisle extended eastward, at a cost of £3,924, defrayed by public subscription : the church was reconsecrated July 22nd, 1887, and has 370 sittings. The register dates from the year 1558. The living is a rectory, average tithe rent-charge £290, gross yearly value, £390, with residence and 28 acres of glebe, in the gift of the trustees of the late Rev. William Powell M.A. and held since 1885 by the Rev. Clement Powell M.A. of Oriel College, Oxford. There is a Baptist chapel. Here is a Cottage Hospital available for seven inmates for diseases not contagious, consumptive, or incurable, and under the superintendence of the rector and supported by voluntary contributions and the patients' fees. Newick Park is the seat of James Henry Sclater esq. D.L., J.P. ; Beechland is the residence of Thomas St. Leger Blaauw esq. J.P. Henry Charles Lane esq. J.P. & James Henry Sclater esq. D.L., J.P. are lords of the manors. The principal landowners are J. H. Sclater esq. D.L., J.P. and Thomas St. Leger Blaauw esq. J.P. The soil is light; subsoil, clay and sand rock. The chief crops are wheat, oats, peas and mangolds. The area is 1,977 acres; rateable value, £4,263 ; the population in 1881 was 1,083.

Parish Clerk, William John Martin.

POST, M. O. & T. O., S. B. & Annuity & Insurance Office.— Frederick Bannister, postmaster. Letters arrive from Cooksbridge S.O. at 8.15 a.m. & 1 p.m.; dispatched at 1 & 5.35 p.m. week days ; & on sunday, arrive at 8.15 a.m.; dispatched at 9.50 a.m

SCHOOLS :—
A School Board of 5 members was formed in 1875 ; W. B. Funnell, clerk to the board ; Alfred Tidy, Newick, attendance officer

Board (infants), built in 1882, at a cost of about £350, for 100 children ; average attendance, 50 ; Miss Emily Baylis, mistress

Charity (girls), founded & endowed by Lady Vernon in 1771, for 12 poor girls of this parish & supported by a rentcharge of £50 a year upon the Park estate ; the school has been certified by the Education Department as sufficient for 56 girls, as a parochial elementary school ; average attendance, 48 ; Miss Mary Ann Dodge, mistress

National (boys), built in 1874, for 150 boys ; average attendance, 60 ; John Oldaker, master

CARRIERS TO :—
BRIGHTON—Thomas Evans & Stephen Grover, every wed. & fri.; Arthur King, every thurs
LEWES—Alfred Coppard, tues. thurs. & sat. & Arthur King, tues. & sat

PRIVATE RESIDENTS.

Blaauw Thomas St.Leger J.P.Beechland
Deacon Mrs. Newick lodge
Gravely Frank, Homelea
Gravely Richard, Greenfields
Keene Commander George Ruck R.N. Ketches
Powell Rev. Clement M.A. Rectory
Powell James, Highhurst
Powell Thomas Baden
RodenClementinaCountess of,North ldg
Rogers Walter Francis, The Point
SclaterJames Henry D.L.,J.P.Newick pk
Sclater Capt.Jas.Rt.Chas.J.P.Newick pk
Shiffner Miss, Ketches

COMMERCIAL.

Avery Henry George, Bull inn
Bannister Frederick, grocer, draper, furniture & earthenware dealer, ironmonger, & post office
Bates William, job master
Brook Jas. Purton, farmer, Goldbridge
Brooks Edward, builder & contractor, Queen's road
Brooks John, sen. builder
Brooks John, jun. bricklayer
Budgen Charles, farmer, Ridgeland
Christmas George Henry, carriage builder & wheelwright
Coppard Alfred, carrier
Cottage Hospital (Richard Gravely M.R.C.S.Eng. medical supt. ; Thomas St. Leger Blaauw, treasurer & sec)

Cox Isaac, carpenter
Day Wm. Geo. market grdnr.Church rd
Dumsday James, tailor
Elphick Joseph, farmer, Church farm
Evans Thomas, carrier
FreelandWm.grocer.drpr.&genl.outfittr
Fuller Ellen (Miss), Henry & Richard, plumbers & painters
Fuller Frederick, boot maker
Funnell William John, surveyor
Funnell W. B. clerk to the school board
Grainger John, bricklayer
Gravely Frank M.R.C.S.Eng. surgeon, Homelea
Gravely Richard M.R.C.S.Eng. surgeon & medical officer of health for the Chailey rural sanitary authority & medical officer, No. 1 district & workhouse, Chailey union
Grover Stephen, fruiterer & carrier
Hammond Joseph, brewer & corn & seed merchant
Hemsley Alfred, baker
Howell Henry, farmer, Broomlye farm
IsardJn.fellmonger,woolstapler&glover
Izard Edmd. frmr.Up.& Low.Birchland
Jenner Norman, butcher
King Arthur, carrier
Knight John, hurdle maker
Martin Ebenezer, farmer, Brett's farm
Martin William John, builder, assistant overseer & parish clerk

Miles James, Crown inn
Millyard Agnes Elizh.(Mrs.),blacksmith
Packham William, tailor, Church road
Pickett John,agent to the Scottish Union & National Insurance Cos
Potter Frederick, gardener to J. H. Sclater esq. Newick park
Rhodes —, farmer, Vuggles
Roser John, blacksmith
Smith Herbert, farmer, Tilehouse farm
Smith Stephen, carrier & farmer, School House farm
Smith Timothy, well sinker
Staplehurst John, beer retailer
Stephens Ernest, farmer, Painter's farm
Swaysland Elizabeth (Miss), ladies' boarding school
Tidy & Son, corn,cake,seed,hay & straw merchants ; agents for artificial manures & Gibbons' ales & stouts
Tidy Alfred, school attendance officer, frmr.&assistant overseer for Fletching
Towner Lewis Arthur, boot maker
Turner Philip & Son, bakers, confectioners & mealmen, Newick green
Turner Benjamin, beer retailer
Turner Henry, shoe maker
Watson Daniel,farmer,Rotherfield farm
Wood Mark, farmer, Ketches farm
Wood Sarah (Mrs.), butcher
Wood Vince, carrier for L. B. & S. C. Railway & coal merchant

Extract from Kelly's Directory 1890

NOVEMBER 1890

Harry Ridley has taken over the licence from Benjamin Turner for The Bricklayers Arms.

Guy Fawkes day was a success with the 'Boys' putting on a fine show. The procession was headed by the Fletching Brass Band with banners, effigies of the Pope and Guy Fawkes, torches, rockets, gaily mounted troopers, jockeys, police and other masqueraders. The route headed from the Bull Inn, past Newick Lodge, Ketches, The Rectory and down Fount Hill where there were loud discharges of gunpowder from the blacksmiths anvils at Mr Roser's forge. The procession continued to Newick Park, with greetings from Mr Sclater, on to Beechlands to see Mr Blaauw, Colonels Bank, Oxbottom, Hollygrove to see Mr and Misses Hughes, The Point, The Rough, the Bricklayers Arms for refreshment, past the Post Office, down to The Green and up to North Lodge and then retracing the steps to the Crown Inn. The fire was lit, the effigies were destroyed and Rule Britannia rounded off the evening with unabated enthusiasm.

The Rev J Wakeford held a mission over a few days with services and sermons to large congregations. The Rev Powell was most grateful to this forceful and powerful speaker.

Parish tithes were paid at the Rectory, collected by the steward H J Powell and his clerk Mr Jackson. The Rev Powell acknowledged the willingness and freedom with which the money was paid. The principal tithe payers were given dinner – James P Brook (Goldbridge), C Budgen, E Izzard (late of Birchlands), E Martin (Home Farm), W J Martin (North Common), R Rhodes (Vuggles), H Smith (Tilehouse), S Smith (School House Farm), T Richards (representing Mr Sclater) and D Watson (Lane End). Other tithe payers were given either a packet of tobacco or tea.

DECEMBER 1890

A special service was held to inaugurate the newly formed Mothers Guild which came about following the November mission by Rev Wakeford. The Association is to foster mutual help and counsel in the bringing up of children to lead a Godly life. Also, a meeting at the Rectory has agreed that a Men's Guild should be formed with members 'to endeavour to lead a Godly, righteous and sober life and to influence others for good.'

A Coal Club meeting was held at the National School. The Club is flourishing with the members making periodic payments to provide for a winter store of coal. Local farmers kindly lend their wagons and horses to deliver the coal. A bonus of four shillings was paid to each member this year.

Captain G Ruck-Keene of Ketches was married in Kensington to Flora Christian the daughter of The Countess Dowager of Roden from North Lodge. Their honeymoon will be in Paris.

On Christmas Eve about 500-700 pounds of free beef was given to the labouring poor of the Parish at the rate of one pound for every member of a poor man's family, all supplied by the two butchers of the village and paid for by the local gentry and others.

The new altar cloth, white embroidered with gold, was used for the first time on Christmas Day.

The Sunday School children had a treat at the National School Room with tea, prizes, presents and a piece of cake and an orange for each child. The main entertainment was a magic lantern show with dissolving views. The event finished with the singing of God Save The Queen.

About 100 people attended the annual ball at the National Boys School Room, dancing through the night and into the morning to the music of Mr Page's band.

The church collections for the year have amounted to £131 17s 0¾d and are distributed to the poor, the Cottage Hospital, Lewes Hospital, foreign missions, home missions, the Chichester Diocesan Association, the Church Building Society, books for the choir and the organ fund.

Cover beating at Newick Park resulted in 20 boys being absent from the National School.

JANUARY 1891

Games of cricket, football and curling were held on the frozen lakes at Sheffield Park. A series of photographs was taken by Mr Hawkins from Brighton. There was also skating on the frozen lakes at Newick Park. Unfortunately a cricket match intended to be played on the Newick Park lake had to be called off because a thaw set in.

The adult members of the church choir had their annual treat at the Rectory with supper, songs and duets.

Newick beat Chailey at whist, the match being held at Mr Bannister's.

FEBRUARY 1891

The Newick Choral Society presented a successful concert of songs and music at the National School.

The juniors of the church choir had a treat at the Rectory with tea, songs, archery, ninepins, halma and other games.

The first monthly meeting of the newly formed Men's Guild at the Rectory classroom got straight down to business with a discussion on gambling, betting and the observance of the Lord's Day.

MARCH 1891

The success of the football club is said to be partly because of the players practising, including on moonlit evenings!

Newick were beating Ringmer 6-1 at football when the game was stopped by mistake 10 minutes too soon. The game then re-started and Newick scored 3 more goals!

Newick's first appearance in a public chess match was against Fletching resulting in a draw. Newick then lost to Fletching in the return match.

The monthly meeting of the Men's Guild in the Rectory classroom discussed the observance of the Lord's Day.

Heavy falls of snow and severe blizzards have caused problems all over Sussex.

William Bates (musician)

William Bates has died. He was the leader of the now defunct Newick String Band and very skilful on the violin. His services were often sought for local concerts and private balls.

The Cottage Hospital annual report stated that 22 patients had been dealt with in the year and that large bills had been incurred for internal repairs. The access is being improved.

A meeting was held to discuss the idea of building a new Reading Room and Coffee Room for the parish. Plans by W J Martin were presented showing a reading room and coffee bar with a games room and bedrooms upstairs for a caretaker and lodgers. It was decided not to have the bedrooms. A site has been offered at only 6 pence per year by Mr Sclater on the understanding that if it was ever given up, the trustees should not use it for any other purpose but it should revert to him, his heirs or assigns. Mr Sclater would not wish to see the building later converted to a shop or anything else which might prove objectionable to people who may buy nearby land for building purposes. Mr Sclater has offered £50 towards the building and Mr Powell has offered £100.

The Rev H M Joseph from Antiqua, West Indies spoke at the National School on behalf of the Society for the Propagation of the Gospel about his work in the West Indies, United States and Canada.

The Ladytide Parish meeting was held in the Bull Inn to elect officers – the overseers of highways, the collector of highway rates and the assessors and collectors of income tax, land tax and inhabited house duty.

The annual Vestry meeting was attended by only four people, apart from the rector. The churchwardens were renominated and the sidesmen appointed.

APRIL 1891

Newick and Chailey Card Club beat the Lewes Conservative Association Card Club at whist. A supper followed in the Bull Inn.

Meetings were held to discuss how to raise money for building the new Reading Room and Coffee Tavern.

The 10 yearly National census was held recording the population of 1033.

The Rev C Powell was presented with a baton in appreciation of his valuable instruction to the Choral Society.

The Choral Society presented a concert of sacred music to an appreciative audience at the National School.

MAY 1891

The cricket club annual meeting was held in the National School with Frank Gravely presiding. The fixtures for the forthcoming season have been arranged.

The Newick Old Benefit Society held their annual event with a procession including the Fletching Brass Band followed by dinner at the Bull Inn. The normal church service was not held this year due to the indisposition of the rector Rev Powell. Sports and entertainment followed in the afternoon and evening including swing boats, shooting saloons, coconut throwing and dancing.

Lord Sheffield's cricket team played at Sheffield Park against an M C C XI which included the renowned W G Grace. Special trains were laid on to bring in visitors from all around. The band of the Inniskilling Dragoons provided music.

JUNE 1891

The Zion Chapel had its 57th anniversary service including refreshments and dinner.

JULY 1891

A confirmation service was held by the Lord Bishop of the Diocese for 41 Newick residents and 31 from Chailey. A striking feature was the large number of adults taking the sacred rite.

Over 40 members of the Basketmakers Arms Birthday Club came to Newick in two four-in-hands for an outing with refreshments, cricket and sports followed by dinner at the Bull Inn.

The Newick Independent United Friends Club had their annual celebrations with business at the Bull Inn, a procession with the Fletching Brass Band, a church service and back to the marquee at the Bull Inn for dinner, dancing and amusements. Rain came into the marquee causing some discomfort.

The employees of Messrs Bryan and Son from Brighton (sign writers, glass embossers and decorators) had their outing to Newick, travelling by road via Offham. They played cricket, engaged in some sports and had a dinner.

Employees of the Bedford Press in London had an outing to Newick with sports and a dinner at the Bull Inn. Many of them returned loaded with flowers.

Philip Turner's boy, playing with matches, created a fire in the stables at the bakers on The Green, burning the straw, cracking the windows and damaging harnesses and equipment.

The choir members had an outing by train to the Naval Exhibition at Chelsea. The displays included a company of Blue Jackets at cutlass and gun drill and torpedo practise on the lake. An armchair from the cabin of The Victory was on view kindly lent by Thomas St Leger Blaauw from Beechlands. The boys also met an old school mate doing duty at the exhibition, now a pupil at the Royal Naval School, Greenwich.

Another annual army volunteers review was held at Sheffield Park with mock battles. The 'defending' force disembarked from the train at Sheffield Park station and marched to Sheffield Park while the 'attacking' force disembarked at Newick and Chailey station and travelled up to Fletching Common, Rotherfield Wood and to the temporary bridges over the River Ouse. Mock hostilities then took place with cavalry, infantry, 16-pounder guns and much noise and activity. Following the battles there was an impressive march past of the forces and the bands, much admired by the invited spectators. Refreshments were taken and then dancing and cheers for Lord Sheffield finished off the day.

AUGUST 1891

Lord Sheffield is annoyed that the London Press chose not to report on last month's volunteer review at Sheffield Park or indeed report on last year's similar event.

The amount of fruit sent away from Newick this season is probably the greatest known. Strawberries in particular are grown more extensively now.

The household furniture and effects from Newick Brewery House have been auctioned.

The boys from the National School had their annual treat at Beechlands before breaking up for the summer holidays – sports, races, swings, see-saws, cricket, tea, prizes and the day finishing with the National Anthem.

SEPTEMBER 1891

The Newick Cottagers Show was held at the National School Room followed by dinner for the judges at The Crown Inn. The prizes for the successful exhibitors are not in money but tickets to exchange for goods in the local shops.

Sir Henry Fletcher MP for the Lewes Division, on his political campaign for the Unionists, gave an address to a large audience at the School Room.

Henry Watts now replaces George Henry Gillham as stationmaster at Newick and Chailey station.

Ernest Stephens is giving up Painters Farm and will be selling the livestock and agricultural implements.

Bretts Farm on The Green is to let now that Ebenezer Martin is quitting the farm. The house, buildings, cottage and the 120 acres is tithe free at a rent of £165 per annum. There will be a sale of the livestock, farm implements and furniture.

OCTOBER 1891

The last cricket match of the season was between the married men and the single men, the marrieds somewhat unusually winning. This was followed by supper at the Bull Inn and the usual formalities of providing details of the state of the club, the seasons results, averages etc. It was stated that if only the club had a better ground the standard of play would be better.

The annual meeting of the Newick Football Club was held with J Oldaker presiding.

Severe flooding occurred along the River Ouse.

NOVEMBER 1891

The gunpowder plot celebrations included a fine procession with a brass band, effigies of Pope and Guy, banners, flaming torches and coloured lights all led by three mounted troopers. The route was to Newick Park, then to the houses of other gentry, the Bricklayers Arms and back to The Green. The bonfire in the middle of The Green was lit with burning of the effigies together with speeches, squibs enlivening the proceedings, dancing, fireworks and the band playing Rule Britannia.

J Pickett died aged 68. He was a member of the church choir for 50-60 years, assistant overseer for 20 years and secretary of the Newick Independent United Friends Club for a long period.

The annual supper of the Bonfire Society was held in the Bull Inn, this time in the commodious new room attached to the house. The balance of the money from the Guy Fawkes celebrations will be given to the Cottage Hospital.

Lord Sheffield has personally promoted and financed a trip to Australia with an England cricket team, including W G Grace. They have now played their first match of the tour.

DECEMBER 1891

Miss Elizabeth Cross is engaged as the sick nurse for the Parish.

George H Gillham, the former stationmaster, was presented with a marble clock by the local inhabitants for his unvarying kindness and courtesy.

The annual ball at the National School was a success with dancing to Mr Page's band and refreshments by P Turner and Son. This event is now recognised as the principal attraction of the season.

A New Year's Eve treat for the Sunday School children was held at the Boys School. Rev C Powell and Mrs Powell provided the entertainment and tea. Prizes were awarded to successful scholars and presents were given to all.

JANUARY 1892

During the Royal funeral of the Duke of Clarence in Windsor the bells of Newick church were tolled and in the evening a muffled peal was rung for one and a half hours.

H D Chrismas completed his apprenticeship at Newick School as a pupil teacher and was given a present by Mr Oldaker, the pupils and scholars – a Gladstone bag. He will now go to Winchester Training College for Teachers.

FEBRUARY 1892

Isabella Shiffner died aged 92 years, the oldest person in the Parish. She was a charitable and self denying supporter of the church living for 32 years at Ketches. She was buried in the family vault at Hamsey. A village meeting was held to discuss how best to commemorate and remember her. A coloured glass window in the church is proposed which could also commemorate Miss Mary Shiffner who died 23 years ago.

A special 'pantomime' train was run to allow visitors to the Brighton pantomime to return to Newick.

The Newick versus Lindfield football match was brought to a premature end when the Lindfield side walked off the pitch in dispute over a foul.

MARCH 1892

Members and friends of the Reading Room club, formed about 5 months ago, had a meeting and a meal with entertainment in the room temporarily rented from Mr Day. Last year's plans for a new Reading Room were abandoned but it is hoped that work will now start on building a new Reading Room.

Newick beat their old rivals Chailey at whist in the Reading Room.

The Rev J D Lord gave a talk in the National School on his missionary work in India.

The Parish meeting at the Bull Inn elected its officers including the overseers and A Tidy as the surveyor who has worked well in keeping the roads in good order.

APRIL 1892

At a special general meeting of Newick Cricket Club it was proposed to change the club's ground from Mitchelswood near The Point, to Mr Wimpress's Home Field at the back of Bretts Farm (at a rent of £6 per year).

Meetings of the Men's Guild in the Rectory Classroom elected officers and also discussed the place and work of the laity in the church.

16 year old Hilda Deacon died of pneumonia.

Mr Sclater has again offered a site for a new Reading Room at a trifling, nominal rent. Plans have been prepared by Messrs Powell of Lewes and tenders invited.

The Cottage Hospital 21st annual report says that 21 patients have been treated over the last year.

The Cricket Club held a concert of music and song at the National School to assist in reducing its current £10 debt.

An epidemic in the village closed the National School for a while.

MAY 1892

After over a year of discussion the new Reading Room is now being built by W J Martin the Newick builder.

The Men's Guild monthly meeting at the Rectory discussed gambling.

Newick Cricket Club is now playing its matches on the new ground at the Home Field. The opening match on a capital wicket was against Horsted Keynes. The annual general meeting re-elected A Tidy as secretary and treasurer and F Gravely as captain for the 9th year. It was agreed to support the giving of a hearty reception to Lord Sheffield when he returns from his Australian cricketing trip.

Henry Prince, the liberal candidate for the Lewes Division, gave an address on The Green speaking on education, Home Rule for Ireland, the land purchase scheme etc.

JUNE 1892

The annual club day of the Newick Old Benefit Society was a great success with a church service, a procession with the Uckfield Brass Band and a dinner in the marquee at the Bull Inn presided over by the Rev C Powell. This was followed by recreation and dancing.

The Earl of Sheffield had his 'welcome home' at Sheffield Park after his Australian cricket tour. His supporters streamed in from all the neighbouring villages.

The Church road laundry staff had a day's outing to Brighton.

JULY 1892

The Newick Independent United Friends Club had their annual club day with formal business, a church service and dinner in a marquee at the Bull Inn, spoilt somewhat by heavy rain coming through the canvas. Sports followed in the afternoon with hurdles, sack race, three legged race, obstacle race, tug-of-war etc with music by the Ardingly Brass Band.

There was a sale of work in three marquees at the Rectory grounds with the £69 proceeds to assist in the furnishing of the new Reading Room. The band of the Chailey Industrial School played under the direction of Mr Glover.

The members of the church choir had their annual outing to London, visiting Westminster Abbey, dinner at Bertrams and then the International Horticultural Exhibition, including Buffalo Bill's Wild West Show at Earls Court.

The annual assembly of volunteer soldiers took place at Sheffield Park over a period of several days, with a tent encampment, assembly of field equipment, military and engineering tasks, experiments with explosives, a parade, regimental sports, tug-of-war, a cricket match etc. Hundreds of spectators attended.

AUGUST 1892

Gen J Ruck-Keene gave a gift of books to the Cottage Hospital in memory of the late Miss J P Shiffner – the bible, Pilgrims Progress, Waverley Novels, Life of Nelson, Life of Wellington and a children's book.

The girls attending the Lady Vernon School had their annual treat courtesy of Mr Sclater who is chairman of the school trustees. 70 of the girls under the charge of Miss Dodge went to Newick Park for games, tea, prizes and presents for each child.

The children of the National School had their annual treat at Beechlands courtesy of Mr and Mrs Blaauw. The children of the Infant School also joined in with the games, egg race, obstacle race and tea. This year there was punting on the lake. The day finished with cheers and the National Anthem.

The Cottagers Garden show was held in the National School.

A horse and cart belonging to the Dowager Lady Roden was left standing but the horse became frightened and ran off. The man in charge tried to stop the horse and got tangled up in the reins and was dragged along. He was shaken and bruised.

SEPTEMBER 1892

Children from Newick joined children from Fletching, Chailey, Danehill and Newhaven for a huge Sunday Schools event at Sheffield Park. 2,000 sat down to tea on a mile length of tables and chairs. The party consumed a massive amount including 300 gallons of tea, 2,000 buns, 185 pounds of butter, 9 hundredweight of cake, 10 bushels of bread and 2 hundredweight of sugar. Music was provided by the Chailey Industrial School Band and the Newhaven Town Band. The Brighton Swimming Club gave a display of diving, swimming and water polo. Daylight fireworks provided more entertainment. The children formed a procession, with banners, singing Onward Christian Soldiers. The whole event was a grand spectacle.

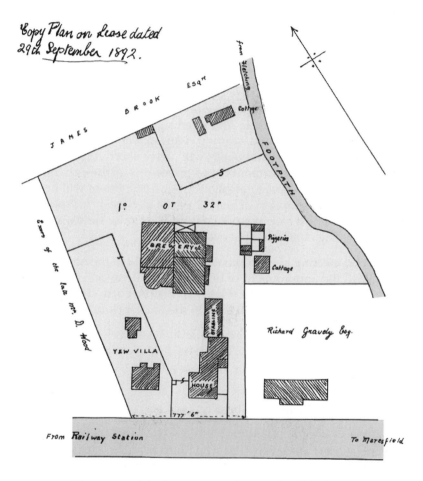

The extent of the brewery premises on the 1892 lease

OCTOBER 1892

The cricket club had their end-of-season supper at the Bull Inn with speeches and toasts. The club has done well this season with batting averages led by E A Smithers, E J Markwick and E A Bailey and bowling by J Wood, A Tidy and G Wood.

A quantity of tools valued at £7-£8 has been stolen from the shop of Isaac Cox the carpenter and joiner.

The Rev Clement Powell has declared the newly completed Reading Room opened. He hopes that it will fulfil its purpose for men to spend their spare hours in the evening and at other times in wholesome recreation and reading. Newspapers, periodicals and games will be provided and books will arrive shortly. It will also be for concerts, entertainments and meetings although not for gambling or for consuming alcoholic liquor. The Room will be open to all with a subscription of only 2 pence per week for members. After the opening a sale of work continued, to raise funds, and then music and song completed the evening.

The annual meeting of the football club was held in the new Reading Room with the appointment of officers. Consideration is now being given to using the Home Field at Bretts Farm for matches. Discussions will need to be held with the cricket club.

The annual harvest home was held at Newick Park for about 40 of Mr Sclater's estate employees with a meal of roast and boiled meats and plum pudding. After the necessary toasts, cricket, games and songs followed.

Mr Hammond's business as brewer, corn and coal merchant is now taken over by E L Brown.

The first concert at the new Reading Room was a great success with music and song and refreshments. W F Ingram is as popular as ever with his comic songs.

NOVEMBER 1892

Large numbers came to this year's Guy Fawkes celebrations despite frequent showers. The procession from the Bull Inn included two horsemen, the Ardingly Brass Band, standard bearers, banners, effigies of Guy and Pope, coloured lights and costumed revellers. The five mile route was a long and weary tramp to Newick Park, Beechland, Holly Grove, Reedens, The Point, The Bricklayers Arms, The Rough and The Crown Inn. The bonfire, 90 feet round, was lit on The Green with speeches, cheers and the band playing.

The Bonfire Society had its annual supper at the Bull Inn with toasts, songs and music courtesy of the host Mr Avery.

DECEMBER 1892

The newly built Mission Hall in Western Road was officially opened with Rev J B Figgis as the preacher. The building, which holds 200, cost £450 to build and was designed by J G Gibbins. It was built by W Wells from Plumpton. The Mission is entirely undenominational with the aim of salvation of souls and the sanctification of believers.

Some coloured glass has been provided in windows in the church in memory of Miss M Shiffner and Miss I Shiffner, ladies known for their acts of charity and religious devotion. Another window is in memory of Miss Hilda Deacon who died in April.

A public auction was held at Goldbridge Farm for the sale of livestock including horses, cattle, two bulls, sows etc together with 50 bushels of apples and agricultural machinery and implements, including wagons, carts, ploughs, a hop presser, harrows and harnesses.

150 scholars of the Sunday School had their annual treat at the National School with tea, Punch and Judy, prizes for attendance and proficiency, sweets and presents for everybody. The event finished with the National Anthem and Mr Oldaker calling for three cheers for the Rev and Mrs Powell.

The church collections for the year have amounted to £111 11s 3¾d for church expenses, providing hassocks, the Diocesan Association, the Church Building Society, home missions, foreign missions, the Church Army, the Cottage Hospital, the Parish Nurse fund and for the poor.

JANUARY 1893

A course of six lectures on sick nursing, arranged by the County Council, has started in the Rectory classroom.

Large numbers of people have been skating on the frozen lakes in Newick Park, even beyond midnight on moonlit evenings, courtesy of Mr Sclater.

Despite wretched weather there was a large audience for the Reading Room concert with songs and music from Rev Sclater, C Sclater, Rev C Powell, Miss M Fitzhugh, Mr Francis, Miss Tidy and Miss Fuller.

The adult members of the church choir had a supper with music at the Rectory courtesy of Rev Powell and Mrs Powell.

FEBRUARY 1893

Newick lost to Uckfield Chess Club, 2½ points to 15½ points. This is the first attempt at chess by the Reading Room members. The visitors greatly admired the appearance and fitting of the new Reading Room.

Thomas Martin was found guilty of being drunk in Newick and fined 5 shillings plus 10 shillings costs.

MARCH 1893

The school board for the Parish has been elected – F Bannister, Henry Howell, Rev C Powell, Captain J R Sclater and a new member, Isaac Cox.

A whist match between 'North' and 'South' was held in the Reading Room.

The Chailey Union suggests that bicycles should now be taxed to help pay for repairs of the highways.

The Ladytide Vestry meeting at the Bull Inn elected officers for the New Year – the overseers, the surveyor of the Parish highways, the collector of highway rates and the collector of assessed taxes. It was agreed that an arrear of poor rate against A E Hobbs, formerly of 'The Retreat' should be recognised as irrecoverable.

Extract from the Minutes of a ———
Meeting of the Guardians of the Chailey Union
held at the Board Room, Union Workhouse,
East Chailington on Wednesday the 1st day
of March 1893

"Resolved — That it is only just that the very
" large number of persons who now use the
" Public Highways on Bicycles and Tricycles
" should contribute in some small degree by
" way of a Tax towards the repair of such
" Highways, which repair at present forms a
" very heavy Charge upon persons engaged in
" Agriculture. That such Tax should be
" applied for the relief of the Local Highway
" authorities repairing such Highways."

"Resolved — Further that all Owners of Bicycles and
" Tricycles should be compelled to register
" their Machines, and that every Owner of
" a Machine so registered, should be ———
" compelled to carry in a conspicuous ———
" position on his Machine, a registered
" number, of sufficient size to be easily ———
" identified by persons passing along the
" Highway."

J. Miles
Clerk of Chailey Union

A proposal to tax bicycles!

125

There are several signatories from Newick on the petition against the Home Rule Bill on the future of Ireland.

Opposite the premises of Fullers, the painters, Mr W Bates's horse and carriage got into difficulties. The reins broke and the horse ran off down The Green, overturning the carriage into a hedge at the back of Mr Freeland's shop. Mr Bates managed to jump clear and was uninjured.

APRIL 1893

The Easter Vestry meeting was held in the church, presided over by the Rev Powell, with the church warden presenting the accounts. A bill from Vince Wood for carrying organ materials should have been paid by Casson and Co, the organ builders, but Casson and Co have ceased to exist. It was agreed that Mr Wood should be paid.

The annual meeting of the Conservative Association elected its officers.

The wind-up football match for the season between Newick village and The Rough was held in the Home Field.

The annual ball, postponed from Christmas, was held at the National School with dancing to Mr Page's band and refreshments by P Turner and Son.

At the annual meeting of Newick Cricket Club officers were elected. It was agreed that T B Powell and the Earl of Sheffield would be patrons.

MAY 1893

Another concert was held at the Reading Room with songs and music.

The old established annual Newick fair had scarcely any business at all this year. It is now in effect just a pleasure fair.

The noble Earl of Sheffield laid on another very successful event at Sheffield Park with his cricket team against the Australians. 18,000 – 20,000 people visited, at times ten to a dozen deep watching the match. A spectacular firework display by C T Brock from Crystal Palace provided much pleasure at a cost of about £500.

Rev Childs from Canada gave an account of his missionary work there.

The late Charles Wallis from Hartfield gave £50 in his will to Newick Cottage Hospital.

Another large annual gathering of volunteer soldiers was held at Sheffield Park over a 3-day period with military manoeuvres, drill, firing exercises, parades and march past.

The Newick Old Benefit Society held its annual event for 70 of its members with dinner in a marquee by the Bull Inn and dancing to the Ardingly Brass Band. Volunteers from the temporary manoeuvres camp at Sheffield Park joined in the amusements in the field.

JUNE 1893

A meeting of the parishioners was held in the Reading Room to discuss how the village should celebrate the forthcoming Royal wedding of the Duke of York and Princess May.

Over three Sundays the church bellringers have been a single family. Edward Brooks with his sons J A Brooks, F E Brooks, K E Brooks, M E Brooks and E W Brooks.

A letter box has been installed in the wall of North Lodge.

Newick National School cricket team beat Chailey National School. A Langridge bowled well for Chailey in the first innings.

JULY 1893

Earnest Backshall, on leaving the Royal Oak public house, was drunk and disorderly on the village green. At court he was fined 5 shillings plus 10 shillings costs.

The festivities for celebrating the Royal wedding of the Duke of York and Princess May were held in the Home Field with flags and bunting and good weather all day long. Fletching Brass Band had a decorated bandstand brightening up the proceedings. A cricket match was played with 20 players per side (married versus singles) followed by luncheon, toasts, a tea for 73 old people of the Parish and tea for 252 children. In the evening there were sports and tug-of-war. Climbing the greasy pole resulted in loud cheers when 14 year old William Elphick climbed it successfully with the help of a piece of string and a pocketful of dust. The day was completed with dancing and singing of God Save The Queen.

The Newick Independent United Friends Club had their 53rd annual business meeting, a church service, a procession with the Fletching Brass Band, dinner, sports and dancing.

A reception was held by Dowager Countess of Hampden at Newick Lodge for the annual meeting of the Mothers Guild, with tea on the lawn, amusements and races.

A festival of choirs of the Rural Deanery of Pevensey III was held in the church with choirs from Newick, Chailey, Fletching, Nutley, East Hoathly, Twyford, Maresfield, Framfield, Uckfield and Danehill.

The annual treat this year for 30 members of the church choir was a trip on the train from Newick and Chailey station to Crystal Palace in London. Fun was had on the switchback railway and the aerial car together with strolling around the grounds, an organ recital, luncheon and tea.

AUGUST 1893

70 girls from the Lady Vernon School, under the charge of the headmistress Miss Dodge, had a treat at Newick Park courtesy of Mr Sclater with games, tea in the open air, prizes together with presents for all. The event was a great success helped by the delightful weather.

A severe outbreak of diphtheria occurred in the village.

SEPTEMBER 1893

Leonard Hemsley is quitting Lower Birchlands Farm and is to auction the stock – 3 cart horses, a cob gelding, dairy cows, steers, heifers, porkers, poultry, farming implements and furniture.

The annual Cottagers Show at the National School exhibited flowers, fruit and vegetables.

T St Leger-Blaauw, the 54 year old son of the late W H Blaauw, has died following his declining health, having spent the last three winters in Bournemouth. He was buried at Newick.

Members of the Reading Room played the Lewes Conservative Association at cards – 6 tables of whist and 1 of cribbage.

The Brighton and District Church Teachers Association had their outing to Newick Park to see the conservatories and alpine garden under the guidance of Mr Sclater's gardener, Mr Potter. This was followed by a business meeting at the National School and then a visit to Shem Weston's Mill Field Tower, now nearing completion opposite the Boys School. There is a fine view from the top of this tall building and a telescope is now installed. The day was completed with a tea at the Bull Inn.

OCTOBER 1893

The Reading Room annual meeting elected officers.

The balance sheet for the Royal wedding celebrations last July has enabled the proceeds to be given to the Cottage Hospital.

The Newick Cricket Club wind-up match at the Home Field was between the over 25's and the under 25's followed by supper at the Bull Inn. T B Powell reminded everybody that on one occasion this summer as many as four Newick XI's were playing on the same day.

Cricket team 1893

The harvest home was held at Newick Park for the employees on the estate with a dinner of roast beef and plum pudding and a cricket match between the 'marrieds' and the 'singles'.

The Newick Football Club annual meeting at the Reading Room elected Thomas Chrismas as secretary and treasurer for the seventh time.

Newick Reading Room defeated Fletching Reading Room in the first game of the chess season. This success may hasten the creation of a chess club at Newick which has long been talked about.

Mrs Doust, the matron and nurse at the Newick Cottage Hospital, resigned and was given a testimonial of a Russian leather purse of money. She has held the post since the hospital started more than 24 years ago and has never ceased to give entire satisfaction. Mrs Jones will take her place as matron.

Five Friendly Societies from Newick, Chailey and Fletching held a parade through Newick – the Newick Old Benefit Society (founded in 1829), the South Saxon Lodge of Oddfellows, the Newick Independent United Friends Club and two others. The procession started at Reedens and marched with banners and the Fletching Brass Band to the church.

NOVEMBER 1893

The Newick Bonfire Society put on a fine display with a procession by the Bonfire Boys including the Ardingly Brass Band, mounted revellers, banners, effigies of Guy Fawkes, the Pope and of Balfour the Rogue who is significant in the Home Rule debate on Ireland. The procession route chosen was shorter than last year's five mile hike. After the procession the bonfire was lit, addresses given and finishing with the firework display and singing of Rule Britannia.

Newick drew 5-5 with Fletching at chess in the Reading Room.

The Newick Bonfire Boys annual dinner at the Bull Inn including singing, toasts, selections from the concertina and a firework display.

Miss Bayliss ceased her appointment at the infants school after 9 years' work. Miss Louisa Depury takes over.

W Grover took over from H Watts as stationmaster.

DECEMBER 1893

The secretary of the Sussex Chess Association, the Rev I W Crosse, played a simultaneous chess match with 13 members of the Newick and Fletching Chess Clubs. He hopes that the Newick club will affiliate with the Association.

Newick beat Uckfield at chess in the Reading Room.

The Newick tradition of giving one pound of beef per head for the poor of the Parish and their families was kept up this year, kindly organised by W J Martin.

Nearly 100 attended the annual ball at the National School Room on Boxing night with dancing to Mr Page's band together with a few tunes on the bagpipes.

The 2nd XI football team managed to draw with Hove Albion on Boxing Day.

The Sunday School children's treat this year at the Boys School included a magic lantern show of stories including Robinson Crusoe and Dick Whittington and his cat. Prizes were awarded to deserving scholars for best attendance etc together with presents and an orange for each child.

JANUARY 1894

Newick beat Nutley at chess in the Reading Room.

A large audience attended the concert in the Reading Room with a programme of high class instrumentals and vocals.

An otter was shot near the Ouse by Mr Howell of Broomlye Farm. The Ouse Angling Preservation Society has given him a reward of £3.

The Rural Sanitary Authority had condemned the insanitary conditions of an open cesspool near the Home Field on Bretts Farm and has therefore devised a drainage scheme for the village. Part of a field owned by Sir Spencer Maryon Wilson is to be considered for irrigation purposes. A meeting of the Newick ratepayers at the Bull Inn discussed whether the scheme was too elaborate for the village but finally approved of the idea.

FEBRUARY 1894

The Southdown Foxhounds met at Newick. A fox was found in Old Park and chased for three hours around the countryside but was then lost.

A special late train on the 15th allowed visitors to get home to Newick from the Brighton pantomime.

Newick drew with Uckfield at chess in the Reading Room.

Mr Godfrey of the Church Defence Institution gave a lecture on the Reformation period of the history of the Church of England with magic lantern views.

The Cottage Hospital produced its annual report showing that 19 patients had been admitted over the year. Mrs Jones has taken over as matron following the retirement of Mrs Doust. The will of Charles Wallis, who did not reside in the neighbourhood, has provided a £50 legacy to the hospital.

MARCH 1894

Newick beat Haywards Heath at chess in the Reading Room.

The Rev Canon Cooper gave an illustrated lecture at the National School on his missionary work in the Fiji Islands and Australia.

The Chailey Union Rural Sanitary Authority annual report refers to the continuing need for adequate drainage to the village.

The Newick 'B' football team lost 1-2 to Hove Albion.

A children's concert of action songs, drill and recitation was given at the Reading Room by the girls of the Lady Vernon School and the infants of the National School under the guidance of Miss Dodge, Miss Depury and Miss Brooke. The event was crowded with many people not able to gain admission.

APRIL 1894

A high class concert of vocals and instrumental music was held in the Reading Room.

Newick Cricket Club held their annual meeting at the National School room.

Sir Spencer Maryon Wilson's keeper Mr Reed caught and killed a large 22 pound otter in a trap at The Hangers by the River Ouse just to the south of Goldbridge. It raised much curiosity as Mr Reed walked through the village carrying his prize.

Newick beat Fletching at whist.

A concert of music, readings and songs in the Reading room was well attended.

The annual livestock fair on the Green attracted little business and even the pleasure fair was a disappointment.

MAY 1894

The game of cricket between Newick and Wivesfield was supplemented by music from the St John's Fife and Drum Band from Brighton who had come to Newick for an outing.

Miss Rose Wood commenced duties as an assistant at the National School.

A quarter of an acre of land is to be kindly given by Richard Archer Ravenhill of Newick Lodge to extend the churchyard eastwards. Some old wooden and brick buildings on the land will be demolished.

Lord Sheffield organised a cricket match at Sheffield Park against the South Africans watched by several thousand spectators. A military band and the Chailey Industrial School band provided music.

The Newick Old Benefit Society had its annual event with business at the Bull Inn, a church service, a procession with the Ardingly Brass Band and a banner proclaiming 'Protection to the Afflicted' followed by dinner, toasts and dancing in the club meadow. A steam switch-back on The Green did a brisk trade.

JUNE 1894

A service was held to commemorate the 60th anniversary of the Zion Chapel in Western Road, followed by a dinner and tea.

71 candidates from Newick and Chailey attended the confirmation service in the church.

A liberal meeting on The Green was addressed by a Mr Osbourne giving a vigorous talk on the Employers Liability bill, Parish Councils, the retirement of Gladstone, the House of Lords etc. Mr T B Powell, in introducing Mr Osbourne, compared the party political process to shearing a pig – plenty of noise but very little wool. This caused plenty of laughter in the audience.

300 scholars and teachers from the Brighton All Souls Sunday School had their summer outing to Newick. They marched from the railway station with their banners and then had tea and recreations at the Home Field.

JULY 1894

Seven houses in Church Road, owned by the late Mrs A H Deacon, are to be sold, including the detached outbuildings and a schoolroom.

The Newick Independent United Friends Club had their annual event with a church service, a parade with the Fletching Brass Band, a dinner in a marquee at the rear of the Bull Inn and sports with obstacle races, three-legged race, potato race, egg race, tug-of-war etc and finally dancing on The Green.

A huge gathering of the Sussex volunteer forces assembled for a military review at Sheffield Park, all by courtesy of the noble and patriotic Earl of Sheffield. 1154 soldiers arrived at Newick and Chailey station as the 'southern' army and 1165 at Sheffield Park station as the 'northern' army. There was great interest shown when the troops arrived at Newick and Chailey station with bands playing and the countryside then resounding to the marching troops heading towards Rotherfield Wood. An amusing incident occurred when one group of 35 (the Lewes Company of the 1st Cinque Ports Rifle Volunteers) arrived at Newick and Chailey station, only to find that their train mistakenly continued on past the station towards Sheffield Park station, where the 'enemy' was due to be! A train came back to Newick and the soldiers disembarked and then double marched to catch up with the rest of the battalion. The two armies approached each other and engaged in mock battles with booming guns on Fletching Common, fighting in Rotherfield Wood, rifles blazing, cavalry charging, defending a bridge built temporarily over the river etc. In the evening when hundreds of spectators were present a march past was arranged in Sheffield Park with soldiers, guns, bands, artillery, horses etc – a wonderful spectacle, with a great ovation for the Earl.

James Miles from The Crown Hotel was fined ten shillings plus ten shillings costs at Lewes Petty Sessions for selling substandard gin.

AUGUST 1894

The churchyard extension was consecrated by the Bishop of Chichester. Part of the old churchyard wall has been demolished and rebuilt, by W J Martin, around the new area with some old gravestones incorporated into the wall.

The Mission Hall Sunday School children had their treat with recreation in the nearby Painters Farm Meadow, tea on the lawn at Mr Avery's house and then prizegiving.

George Varnham was found lying in the road in a drunken state by police constable Pocock. He has now been fined five shillings at Lewes Petty Sessions.

The girls of the Lady Vernons School had a treat under the guidance of the headmistress Miss Dodge and the assistant Miss Turner. Tea was taken on the lawn at Newick Park followed by amusements, races, prizes, presents for all and voting for the annual good conduct prize.

Infants from the National School had a tea with games and presents all under the guidance of the mistress Miss Depury.

SEPTEMBER 1894

The boys of the National School had a treat at the Rectory with cricket, rounders and tea finishing with singing of God Save The Queen.

The Cottage Garden Show was held in the National School Room with 186 entries followed by dinner for the officials at The Crown Inn courtesy of Mrs Miles. Prizewinners were Stephen Brown, Robert Booker, John Parsons, Benjamin Martin, James Wheatland (senior and junior), Norman Jenner, George Kingsland, Thomas Smith, George Homewood, William Martin, William Tingley, John Mainwood, Thomas Hodges, William Smith, Thomas Martin, Agnes Brooks, Ernest Brooks, John Hill, Widow Hodges and Alfred Hodges.

The farmer John Colman, having allowed 5 of his cows to stray on the highway in August, was fined 6 pence for each cow plus 8 shillings costs at Lewes Petty Sessions.

The church choir had an outing to London with a trip on the Thames, a visit to London Bridge, the new Tower Bridge and the Tower of London, dinner at Cannon Street Hotel and a service at St Paul's Cathedral.

The Newick and Chailey Friendly Societies had their annual parade assembling near the Point and then walking with the Ardingly Brass Band down Western Road to The Green, to the church for a service, to the Post Office, The Rough and along to Reedens.

OCTOBER 1894

Henry W Smith from Chailey was fined 10 shillings at Lewes Petty Sessions for being drunk in Newick in September.

The harvest home for Mr Sclater's workmen was held in Newick Park with dinner, toasts, cricket between the marrieds and the singles and singing of old country songs. John Martin's rendering of Old John Barleycorn was especially appreciated.

NEWICK FOOTBALL XI

G.Watts. J.Farley. F.Watts. E.Warnett. F.Pettit. T.Wheatland. G.H.Chr
J. Wood. W.Diplock. C.Grainger. H.Streater
J. Bates   CAPT. — Elphick

Newick football team 1894

A concert at The Reading Room comprised nearly all the performers being from Newick with songs, music and recitations.

At the football club annual general meeting in the Reading Room members were informed of the notice to quit the field at Bretts Farm formerly rented from Mr Wimpress. The club secretary was empowered to try and find another ground elsewhere.

The Rev E J Grosse played 9 games of chess at the same time against Newick players.

George Anscombe was fined 10 shillings at Petty Sessions for being drunk in Church Road.

NOVEMBER 1894

Prizes were awarded at The Rectory classroom for the best entries in the September Cottage Garden Show.

The Guy Fawkes celebrations included a procession with the Fletching Brass Band from the Bull Inn to the Rectory, to the Rough, High Hurst, Holly Grove and Western Road. Effigies of the Pope and guy were hauled to the top of the bonfire. After all the recent rain, paraffin and tar barrels did not assist greatly in getting the bonfire burning, so it only burned slowly.

A jumble sale in the Reading Room raised £22, part of which will be in aid of the Parish lending library which has operated from the Rectory for 9 years.

The Newick Choral Society, which was successful a few years ago, is to be re-established with practices commencing immediately.

Newick beat Nutley at chess in the Reading Room.

The Bonfire Boys had their annual supper at The Bull Inn culminating in the usual firework display.

Councillor Thompson from Richmond, Surrey gave a talk at the National School on the objects of the new Local Government Act. The Act provides for the creation of Parish Councils.

DECEMBER 1894

There was good attendance to the poll at the National School for election of nine Parish Councillors. Those elected are M V Wood, F Bannister, J Oldaker, Rev C Powell, J W Isard, H Howell, W G Powell, J Smith and C King.

Alfred Tidy has recently married so this was a fitting time to give him recognition for his valuable service to the cricket club as secretary and treasurer. He was presented with a gold watch and chain.

At Lewes Petty Sessions Alfred and Amos Williams, labourers from Chailey, were given prison sentences of one month for poaching on Mr Budgen's land.

The Sunday School children had a treat at the National School on Boxing Day with entertainment from Professor Heno conjurer and ventriloquist from Brighton. This was followed by tea, prizes and presents for all.

The annual ball was held at the National School with over 100 attending, dancing to Mr Page's band till morning.

JANUARY 1895

The first meeting of the Parish Council for Newick was held at the National School attended by over 50 ratepayers. Rev C Powell was elected chairman, W J Martin as clerk and F B Whitfield as treasurer. A further meeting discussed custody of the Parish books and documents and recognised that allotments were required for the village.

The gardener Thomas Hodges was given a caution at Lewes Petty Sessions for being drunk in Church Road on Boxing Day.

Sir Henry Fletcher, the Member of Parliament for the Lewes division, gave a speech in the Boys Schoolroom on Home Rule for Ireland, the Local Government Act etc.

The Coal Club was reorganised this month.

Newick played Uckfield at chess in the Reading Room. The result was a draw 4-4.

The National School received a contribution of £5 17s 0¾d from last year's church collection.

The members of the Reading Room challenged the non-members to whist.

FEBRUARY 1895

A cricket match was played on the frozen lake at Sheffield Park. Lord Sheffield also organised a skating exhibition on the lake with championship skaters James Smart and Hendrich Lindahl showing their racing skills.

The rector's cousin G H Powell gave a lecture in the Reading Room on progress and democracy.

Walter Powell Colman was knocked down by a horse drawn omnibus in Newick Rough Road. At the assizes he was awarded £20 damages.

The Cottage Hospital produced its 24th annual report showing that 21 patients have been treated over the last year. The matron's sitting room has been refurbished this year.

The Newick Choral Society gave a concert of music and song in the Reading Room. Over 20 voices were in the choir. The proceeds will go to the Reading Room and to the Choral Society.

MARCH 1895

A block of 3 freehold cottages abutting The Green, owned by the late John Leney, was purchased by Miss Veness, one of the tenants, for £530.

A measles epidemic closed the National School.

The Parish Council appointed assessors and collectors of taxes for the ensuing year and also discussed allotments and recent election expenses.

In the annual report of the Medical Officer of Health for the Chailey Rural District Council the need for better drainage to the village is repeated again.

APRIL 1895

The Royal Oak Slate Club and the Brighton Arms Slate Club played a football match at High Hurst. The result was 4-4, being a game more for entertainment than of high quality skills. A large amused crowd watched.

The whist championship at the Reading Room was won by A Tidy and M V Wood.

Although the Parish Council has only just been formed the Council's annual meeting was held in the Boys School. The Rev C Powell was re-elected as chairman and overseers were appointed.

A pigeon shooting match with Mr Carlsden and his friends was held in the field behind the Bull Inn, attracting a large number of spectators.

The annual Eastertide Vestry meeting at the Rectory classroom is now simply for ecclesiastical affairs as the new Parish Council is dealing with other Parish matters.

The tenancy of the Home Field for the cricket club has, since the end of last season, ceased. A new ground has been found – the old workhouse field owned by Sir Spencer Maryon-Wilson. The ground has been prepared with the pitch levelled, rolled and seeded.

An impromptu concert of songs and readings was held in the Reading Room, arranged by G H Powell. The proceeds will be for the Reading Room fund.

The licence for The Royal Oak has been transferred from John Staplehurst to Matilda Staplehurst.

The livestock fair on The Green had little trading this year but the swings, roundabouts, shooting galleries, coconut throws etc provided a popular, brisk trade.

A fashionable wedding took place with Miss Deacon from Beechlands marrying Colonel Spratt.

MAY 1895

The new cricket ground at the old workhouse field is now in use.

The Parish Council meeting agreed to seek approval from the Lord of the Manor for the Parish Council to take over control of Newick Green – particularly to be able to control the nuisance caused by the caravan gypsies who assemble there on fete and fair days. The meeting agreed to form a Committee to consider footpaths in the Parish. The existing allotments near the Boys School and at Colonels Bank were the subject of discussion.

The Newick Old Benefit Society had its annual business at the Bull Inn followed by a church service, a procession with the Fletching Brass Band, dinner in a marquee and then amusements – a switchback railway was an immense attraction being an innovation for Newick.

JUNE 1895

The Zion Chapel had its 61st anniversary.

A musical recital with organ and violin was held at the church.

The Newick brewery has now been sold comprising the brewery, two villas and two cottages.

Postcard of the village green

Walter Larkin is objecting to the Chailey Rural District Council wishing to take part of his farmland for the sewage outfall.

History is made this month. The Rev William Heale has scored an all-time record for a Newick batsman of 171 runs at the cricket match between Newick and Horsted Keynes. Surely that will not be beaten for many a year.

JULY 1895

The Newick Independent United Friends Club annual meeting was held with dinner in a marquee at the Bull Inn. The event included a procession with the Fletching Brass Band together with a fete, coconut throws, swings etc and dancing.

The Evangelization Society held a mission in a tent off Church Road.

The newly formed Sheffield Arms cricket club played their first match at Newick. J Langridge performed well for Sheffield Arms but they were beaten by Newick.

A hay rick owned by S Wood and Sons, in a meadow on the Beechlands Estate, was set alight by two little boys. Earnest Best and George Goddard in their brewers dray, on the way home to

Cooksbridge Brewery, tried to put out the flames. Up to 100 other helpers joined in carrying buckets of water from the ditch at the bottom of the hill. In the excitement somebody fell in the ditch. The banks of a lake at Beechlands were breached to provide some water into the ditch. The Uckfield Fire Brigade were telegraphed and came to assist and eventually the blaze was extinguished. 30 tons of hay were rendered unfit for use.

Another review of volunteers was held at Sheffield Park with 2,500 officers and men and a mock battle on Chailey Commons. Four special trains brought some of the participants to Newick and Chailey station with their artillery, ammunition wagons and baggage. Others went to Sheffield Park station. The event finished with a march past, tea and cheers for Lord Sheffield.

AUGUST 1895

The sergeants mess of the 1st Sussex Artillery Volunteers from Brighton travelled to Newick and Chailey station and then walked to Newick for a treat at the Bull Inn – dinner, cricket, bat and trap and a drive and ramble around the countryside.

The children from the National School had their annual treat in the grounds of the Rectory with the Rev Powell and Mrs Powell. Tea was taken in the avenue followed by games, races and prizes.

SEPTEMBER 1895

New coloured glass was inserted in the window in the north side of the chancel of the church to the memory of the late Mr Blaauw. It shows the annunciation of the Virgin Mary.

The concert at the Reading Room to raise funds comprised all performers from Newick.

Harvest Thanksgiving was held at the Zion Chapel. The Chapel used to be attended by large congregations but attendance is now declining.

The Parish Council meeting at the school discussed the problem of still finding land for allotments. Also, footpaths need repairing – the one near the brewery leading to Fletching and the one between The Rough and Ketches. The Council is considering acquiring The Green.

The Reading Room annual general meeting appointed its officers.

OCTOBER 1895

The Newick Cricket Club wind-up match for the season was played between the marrieds and the singles. The annual supper followed in the evening at the Bull Inn courtesy of the landlord Mr Avery. E J Markwick received two silver cups for best bowling average. Songs were sung and the appropriate toasts made including a toast to F Gravely who has been the captain since the club's formation in 1884. Mr Tidy, the secretary, is hopeful that the club will raise money at forthcoming concerts for improvements to the new ground.

A chess match was held for the 3rd successive year in the Reading Room with the Rev E I Grosse, secretary of the Sussex County Chess Association, playing simultaneous matches on 7 boards with Newick players. Newick lost 3-4.

John Smith caught influenza, weakened and died. He was a Parish Councillor, was involved with the Coal Club and was popular amongst the working classes.

The harvest home was held at Newick Park with 40 employees sitting down to a dinner of roast beef and plum pudding in the granary. Captain Sclater presided. This was followed by cricket, tea and songs. The weather kept fine all day long.

The court in Lewes fined Jesse Read £2 or, in default, 3 weeks imprisonment for stealing 2 pheasants from Walter Larkin.

The football club annual general meeting appointed its officers. Club football has now firmly taken its place in the social life of the village following its beginnings simply as a local amusement indulged in by grammar school boys, youths and their elders.

Newick Reading Room lost to Lewes Conservative Club at whist.

NOVEMBER 1895

The Bonfire Society Guy Fawkes celebrations were marred somewhat this year by persistent rain. The procession with the

Newick Drum and Fife Band included guys, torches, coloured lights, effigies of Pope and Guy and banners proclaiming 'Long Live Our Protestant Queen', 'Cheer Boys Cheer', 'Success to the Newick Bonfire Society' and 'Girls Be True To Your Bonfire Boys'. There were fewer spectators than normal watching the bonfire.

A whist match was held between the married members of the Reading Room and the singles.

The Parish Council meeting was held in the Boys School discussing repairs to the footpaths across Goldbridge Farm and near Ketches.

The County Football Association says that the rules have been broken when Newick played Nutley because the Nutley Club was unaffiliated.

The jumble sale at the Reading Room to clear the debt of the building fund raised £30-£40.

DECEMBER 1895

The Parish Council meeting agreed the East Sussex County Council's new basis for the County rate assessment.

Another whist match was held between the married and singles of the Reading Room. Newick also beat Chailey 14-11.

The Royal Oak Slate Club had their 2nd annual supper.

The annual ball was held at the Boys School on Boxing night with dancing to Mr Page's band until 5 o'clock in the morning.

The Sunday School children had a tea at the National School with prizes awarded. Each child took home a present, an orange and a piece of cake.

JANUARY 1896

The concert at the School Room, arranged by the Cricket Club, raised £10.

Newick drew with Nutley at chess in the Reading Room.

The church choir adults had a supper and musical evening.

Newick lost to Fletching at whist in the Reading Room.

A concert in the Reading Room for the Reading Room funds was very popular.

The bell ringers had their annual supper at The Rectory.

FEBRUARY 1896

T B Powell won at the chess tournament in the Reading Room.

A missionary meeting was held at the Boys School with an address by the Rev J J Priestly on his work in Bombay.

Newick played Barcombe at a games tournament comprising 20 players on each side with chess, draughts, bagatelle, cribbage and whist. Newick won 27½ points to 25½ points with a decisive success at draughts.

The concert at the Boys School, on behalf of the Cricket Club, raised £7 to meet the expenses for levelling and re-turfing the new cricket ground.

The 'Newick Reading Room' lost to the 'Cliffe Parish Room' at whist.

MARCH 1896

An auction was held for the freehold of the Newick brewery estate comprising the brewery, two villas and two cottages.

Newick beat Fletching 8-1 at a bagatelle contest.

'Newick Reading Room' beat 'Barcombe Reading Room' at a return games tournament of chess, whist, cribbage and bagatelle – 23½ points to 17½ points.

The new cricket pitch at the old workhouse field has now been re-laid and enlarged. It is an immense improvement so some admirable wickets are anticipated this forthcoming season.

The annual report by the Medical Officer of Health for the Chailey Rural District Council refers to the continuing need for better drainage to the village. There are still complaints regarding the offensive smells, including from the cesspit which serves the houses on either side of the Crown Inn and the laundry.

The Parish Meeting at the Boys School nominated collectors of land and income tax and inhabited house duty for the ensuing year.

APRIL 1896

Parish Councillors have been elected following the poll at the Boys Schoolroom.

The Cricket Club held their annual general meeting at the Boys School.

The Vestry meeting elected its officers.

Newick beat Fletching at chess in the Reading Room.

The Ladies Social Club held an evening of dancing at the Rectory.

A concert was held in the Reading Room

The annual fair was held on The Green. Buying and selling livestock is still continuing to decline. The whole Green was occupied by caravans with their occupants and accessories many of whom stayed for three days.

Thomas Baden Powell was fined 5 shillings for having an unmuzzled dog.

MAY 1896

Percy Gravely had a picture exhibited at the Royal Academy exhibition entitled 'Rescuing Cattle from a Flood in the Ouse Valley'.

A concert at the School on behalf of the Teachers' Benevolent and Orphan Fund was well attended.

E. Isard's butchers shop with Ebenezer Isard, his sister and a delivery boy. Rump steak was 1s per pound and top side of beef 9d per pound.

The village green before the erection of the village pump

Two gypsies, Henry Slender and John Britton, were fined at Lewes Petty Sessions for allowing horses to stray in Newick.

Crowds of 30,000 people flocked to see the Prince of Wales at Sheffield Park where Lord Sheffield's XI, under the captaincy of W G Grace, met the Australians for two days of cricket. This was a splendid event with lovely weather and the grounds looking beautiful with the flowers, trees, lakes and waterfalls. The Prince arrived by train to Sheffield Park station where the 1st Sussex Engineers band played, followed by a drive to Lord Sheffield's grounds in a state carriage and four grey horses. The route was decorated with arches of roses and there was loud cheering all the way. A photograph of the Prince and Lord Sheffield was taken. Children had the day off school.

The Newick Old Benefit Society held its annual dinner at the Bull Inn. The Ardingly Brass Band played. Details were read out on the payments made to sick members, pensioners, the Medical Officer and for funerals etc.

JUNE 1896

Walter F Larkin, the tenant of Goldbridge Farm, had a serious accident while filling a water cart from a pond. He was dragged along for 30 yards under his cart when the horse moved off and when the wheel passed over him he received a fractured arm and ribs and a wound to the head. He was attended to by Richard and Frank Gravely.

JULY 1896

The Newick Independent United Friends Club had their annual event at the Bull Inn. Following a toast to F Gravely he responded by saying he was always pleased to do what he could for the Club but there was one thing medical men had not been able to cope with and that was old age and decay – however, perhaps as the world was now getting so advanced they might be able to discover some remedy even for that. He thanked members for drinking his health.

14 men from the Lion Slate Club from Hove had an excursion to Newick which sadly went wrong. After leaving the Bull Inn their waggonette

with a pair of horses turned too quickly, broke a wheel and tipped over. The party had to return to Brighton by train.

The church choir had their summer outing this year to the Indian Exhibition at Earls Court in London. The big wheel created great amusement.

Walter Larkin from Goldbridge Farm died from the injuries he received in June.

The Ladies Social Club had a well attended sale of work in the Rectory grounds with toys, a rummage stall, sweets, fancy stall, new garments, a dipping bag and refreshments. The £17 proceeds will help towards buying a piano for concerts.

AUGUST 1896

The Rev C Powell, as president of the Newick Football Club, presented a silver watch and chain to T Chrismas in recognition of his services to the club. He took a leading part in the formation of the club in 1887 and has been involved as secretary and in the management of the club since then.

The Girls Friendly Society of the Western Branch of the Rural Deanery of Pevensey had its annual festival in Newick. 155 girls assembled in F Gravely's meadow opposite Newick Lodge and played stoolball, rounders etc and had tea. The Chailey Industrial School Band provided music.

SEPTEMBER 1896

The Cricket Club annual supper at the Bull Inn was preceded by the 'wind-up' match between 'The Radicals' and the Conservatives.

The meeting of the Parish Council at the National School discussed the question of acquisition and full control over The Green which at present is vested in the Lord of the Manor.

OCTOBER 1896

The members of the Reading Room held their annual general meeting showing that the balance sheet is satisfactory.

The Friendly Societies of the Parish held a parade joined by the Foresters from Chailey and the Ardingly Brass Band.

The Chailey Rural District Council discussed the problem of storm water in Blind Lane.

NOVEMBER 1896

The Lord of the Manor has appointed the Parish Council as his deputy for The Green. Copyholders will maintain their rights.

Bonfire night was a great success with processions, a band, torches, effigies of the Pope and Guy Fawkes, banners, a brightly decorated car, squibs, crackers, wheels and the bonfire. A grand display of fireworks was provided by Captain Harcourt Rose at Beechlands.

A burglary occurred at Bannisters, the grocers, drapers and post office, with the loss of parcels worth £5-6 and a pound packet of tobacco.

The Mission Hall was broken into and some wine drunk. Some money boxes were broken into but there was no money in them anyway.

The Bonfire Supper was held at the Royal Oak Inn attended by about 40.

A meeting held at the Boys School has decided to form a liberal organisation to be called the Newick Liberal and Radical Association.

Ernest Backshall was fined 10 shillings at Lewes Petty Sessions for being drunk and disorderly at Newick.

DECEMBER 1896

Brighton Foot Beagles met at Goldbridge and found several hares. One was chased and swam across the River Ouse which was overflowing its banks from the recent storms. The beagles followed. The party then went to Mr Kenward's house.

The Uckfield Fire Brigade were called to a fire at Newick Park.

The Royal Oak Slate Club held its annual supper with about 50 attending.

The girls of the Lady Vernon School had their annual treat with tea, presents from the Christmas tree and prizes to the top girls in each class. The children also provided an entertainment in the evening under the guidance of Miss Dodge the mistress and Miss Price her assistant.

T B Powell played simultaneous chess matches against members of the Fletching Chess Club and won 8-1.

The annual ball was held in the Boys School as usual with Mr Page's Quadrille Band from Lewes providing the music. This event, first started 10 years ago, is now recognised as the most attractive and enjoyable of the winter season in Newick.

JANUARY 1897

Thomas Luckens from Newick was sued by William Gilbert for outstanding rent at Lewes County Court.

Newick had an easy victory over Fletching at whist in the Reading Room. Later, the 'singles' beat the 'marrieds'.

Land has now been reserved on Goldbridge Farm for a sewerage outfall to serve the village.

FEBRUARY 1897

The church choir enjoyed the hospitality of the rector and his wife when they were given supper at The Rectory. The church bell ringers were guests at a later gathering.

The Southdown foxhounds met on The Green with several Newick tradesmen there. After chasing over Newick Park, Beechlands and Founthill Wood a fox was caught at Hanger Wood near Goldbridge.

A concert of vocal and instrumental music in the Reading Room was a great success.

W H Freeland (junior) had his wedding celebration at the Bull Inn with about 50 guests – a good time was had by all.

The Weald of Sussex Habitation of the Primrose League had a crowded meeting in the School Room with a talk on education and the principles and work of the League. Sir Henry Fletcher spoke on the Agricultural Rating Bill and the Fletching Drum and Fife Band provided some musical selections.

A cricket club concert of music and song by Miss Tidy, Rev C Powell, Miss Rogers, C Pickett, F Bailey, Mr Parker, Mr C Francis and comic singer Mr Woodriffe, raised £11.

George Salvage and Ernest Backshall were fined at Lewes Petty Sessions for being drunk and disorderly and fighting on The Green.

A meeting in aid of the Society for the Propagation of the Gospel was presided over by the Rev Powell with the guest being Rev Canon Cooper speaking on his missionary work in Africa.

Newick beat Nutley at chess in the Reading Room.

Newick lost to St Michael's Social Club (Lewes) at whist in the Reading Room.

The Cliffe Parish Club from Lewes beat Newick at a games contest of whist and cribbage in the Boys School.

The Newick Parish Council meeting at the Boys School discussed Indian Famine Relief, the poor state of the footpath from The Green to Fletching, the dangerous stile on the path from The Rough to Cornwells Bank, the spring on The Green and the powers of control over The Green whereby the Parish Council will act as the Lord of the Manor's lawful deputy in certain matters.

Lewes Police Court considered the case of the riotous behaviour by a group of men from Barcombe outside Founthill Farm where stones were thrown, windows and tiles and a lamp broken and threats were made to William Hodges. The men were fined.

John Elliot from Hove suffered from a bad heart and died when he fell in Newick Station goods yard while loading straw from a truck.

MARCH 1897

There is some local opposition to the plans for a drainage scheme for the village. Some villagers feel that ratepayers money should not be spent on solving the problem because it is the fault of the wealthy landowners for not properly disposing of sewage from their properties and their tenants properties. This was said as long ago as April 1874. Bye-laws exist and should be enforced for the proper cleaning out of earth closets, privies, ashpits and cesspools.

Miss Deborah R Cornwell has taken over from Miss Depury as infant school mistress.

The Parish meeting appointed assessors and collectors of taxes for Newick.

APRIL 1897

The Parish Council election poll was held at the Boys School.

The Cricket Club annual meeting was held in the Boys School showing a satisfactory balance sheet. Mr Ravenhill was elected secretary and treasurer.

The church now has a new gilded and painted reredos greatly enriching the chancel. It was designed by the Rev C Powell's cousin Charles Powell and shows the Lamb of God and biblical figures.

The church reredos

The Easter Vestry meeting elected the church warden, sidesmen etc.

The annual fair on The Green now has almost no livestock sales. The other amusements are taking over, the main feature being Harris's fair with a roundabout driven by steam power and illuminated by electricity.

The Chailey Rural District Council has now approved plans for the drainage system for the village.

A well attended meeting at the Boys School considered what should be done in the village to celebrate Queen Victoria's Diamond Jubilee. One idea was for providing lamps through the village but this was rejected. Indeed the provision of gas lamps, with a little gas works for the village, was also discussed as long ago as July 1871. Another idea for the Jubilee was for a free bed to be provided at the Cottage Hospital but this was also rejected. The popular idea is for a pump to be erected on The Green, to have some sports and a tea provided.

H C Lane, the Lord of the Manor, approves of the idea of having a pump, provided the copyholders have no objection.

MAY 1897

A concert of classical music and vocals was held in the Reading Room.

The Local Government Board Inspector held a public inquiry at the Newick Boys School into the application by Chailey Rural District Council for permission to borrow £1329 for providing a sewage disposal scheme for the village. The inspector heard the case for and against the scheme.

The Ladies Social Club held a successful, well attended dance.

W R Hodges of Founthill Farm was summoned by his wife for desertion but the court determined that there was insufficient evidence that any order should be made.

The Parish Council agreed that a pump should be erected on The Green to celebrate the Jubilee. Mr T W Freeland does not wish to see cart washing there when the pond is dry. T Evans wants to be sure that any water troughs to be provided at the pump can be regularly drained otherwise horses could bring disease such as glanders into the water and the disease could be passed on.

A well attended concert was held at the Reading Room for the benefit of Mr C Francis the local comedian who has regularly amused audiences here for several years.

The Royal Oak public house team played on The Green against a team from the Lamb public house, Piltdown. The Royal Oak lost 1-3.

The Newick Liberal and Radical Association held a public meeting in the Schoolroom with addresses by Julius Bertram, C H Corbett and Lindsay Brown.

JUNE 1897

The Newick Old Benefit Society and the Newick Independent United Friends Club held their annual event with business at the Bull Inn, a procession with the Ardingly Brass Band, a church service and dinner in a marquee back at the Bull Inn. This is the first time the two societies have had their feasts on the same day.

A Victoria Jubilee mug

Queen Victoria's Diamond Jubilee was a splendid celebration. Flags, ensign and bunting were everywhere including in the trees. Banners proclaimed good wishes to the Queen and the Royal Family. Church bells were rung. Following a muster around the Royal Standard on The Green with singing of the National Anthem a procession marched off with W Packhams Newick Drum and Fife Band to the cricket field. Sports were held with races, kicking a football, egg-and-spoon race, sack race, hurdle race, slow bicycle race, long jump, high jump, tug-of-war and climbing the greasy pole for a leg of mutton – all for prizes to be won. The prizes were not money but tickets to exchange for anything to the value stated at any shop in Newick. Free teas and other refreshments were provided by A Hemsley and P Turner in a long range of tea tents. Every child received a Jubilee mug. Those old and infirm who could not leave their homes were given a parcel of tea and cake. The Bonfire Boys provided a torchlight procession to The Green lighting the 25-30 feet high bonfire and firing off 60 sky rockets. Loyal singing of the National Anthem was led by the rector and there were three cheers for the Queen. Also a hearty cheer was given for P H Hare for organising the event so well. More music and fireworks followed and another torchlight procession went around the village. Several fire balloons were sent up and more rockets. Wonderful weather held out for the whole day. A day never to be forgotten. God Save The Queen.

Too much beer was ordered for the Jubilee. It took 2 or 3 subsequent evenings to consume the surplus.

The Local Government Board has approved Chailey Rural District Council's drainage scheme and authorised a loan of £1329.

JULY 1897

Eli Hollingdale has taken over as stationmaster from William Grover.

AUGUST 1897

Messrs Dutton and Thorowgood, boot and shoemakers from Brighton, had an outing to Newick with sports, a quoit match and a dinner.

The church choir had an outing to the Victorian Exhibition at Earls Court.

SEPTEMBER 1897

The cricket club purchased a mower from the blacksmith Mr Croucher for £4 8s 3d.

Lewes magistrates have dismissed the case involving a quarrel at Woodbine Farm between James Perring and his sister Elizabeth Nicholas.

The Parish Council meeting at the Boys School Room discussed the need for a better postal service.

A well attended concert of songs and music was given at the Boys School Room for the benefit of the Newick Drum and Fife Band. A mandolin was played which has not been heard here before.

Elizabeth Anscombe was found dead having drowned in the pond on Fletching Common. She was aged 59. Until a few months ago she had worked at the refreshment bar in Newick and Chailey station.

OCTOBER 1897

At the well attended harvest thanksgiving a collection was taken to pay for the cost of new chancel lamps and for the Cottage Hospital.

The annual general meeting of the members and subscribers of the Reading Room was held showing a satisfactory balance. Officers were elected. Consideration is being given to providing a billiard table.

The Newick Cricket Club had their annual wind-up supper at the Bull Inn. G Tidy was presented with a prize bat for the best batting average.

F Bannisters grocers and drapers shop is advertising souvenirs of Queen Victoria's long reign.

The Newick Liberal and Radical Association held a public meeting in the Schoolroom with Capt the Hon T S Brand talking on the Liberal policy and C J Whitting discussing current topics notably Lord Salisbury's foreign policy and registration reform.

NOVEMBER 1897

The Guy Fawkes celebrations were larger than usual this year. Effigies of the Pope and Guy were displayed in the procession together with banners and an illuminated car. Squibs, crackers and noisy rousers enlivened the proceedings with the Fletching Brass Band playing the music and two mounted horsemen joining the march. The procession route visited the premises of the principal subscribers – The Dowager Countess of Roden at North Lodge, Mr R Gravely, Mr F Gravely, Mr Ravenhill, Rev C Powell, Mr Rogers at The Point, Mr Hughes at Holly Grove, Mrs Hallett at Reedens, Mr Manwaring at The Rest and others. The bonfire blazed with the effigies being consumed in the flames and a display of sky rockets and wheel rockets impressed the crowds.

78 year old J H Sclater died. He was a well known and beloved figure in the village and one of the oldest magistrates in the County. His funeral, with the coffin drawn on an open hearse, was a sad impressive scene. Blinds were drawn in almost every house and cottage in the village.

James Henry Sclater

The sewage works for Newick has finally been commenced. Dr Gravely has been pleading for this since 1874.

The rent audit and dinner for the tenants of Beechland estate was held at the Crown Inn.

Newick played whist at Lewes against the Lewes Conservative Club.

The Parish Council discussed the path from The Point to Oxbottom and will ask Mr Bigge to erect a fence for protection of the path.

The Newick Bonfire Society had its annual supper at the Royal Oak with toasts, songs and entertainment from the Newick and Chailey String Band. G Norman presided.

A Parish meeting was held at the Boys School to discuss the Local Government proposal to amalgamate the Chailey Union with Lewes Union and part of the West Firle Union. The opinion of the meeting was to protest at the proposal.

DECEMBER 1897

Newick beat Fletching at whist in the Reading Room in the first match of the season.

Captain James Robert Charles Sclater of Newick Park died after catching a chill last month at his father's funeral.

Over 100 children assembled at the National School Room for a Sunday School treat with tea, prizes for attendance and proficiency and a present or a parcel of clothing for each child.

Newick Reading Room played Nutley at chess and whist.

The drainage works for the village are progressing.

JANUARY 1898

A Parish Council meeting was held at the Boys School. A suggestion from A Martin that a bathing facility should be provided on the River Ouse will be considered. Mr Tidy has agreed to repair the fence running between The Point and Oxbottom. The meeting expressed its condolences to the Sclater family for their recent loss.

Newick Reading Room team lost to the Lewes Reading Room team at cribbage and whist.

The annual general meeting of the Newick Liberal and Radical Association was held in the Boys School Room. Officers were elected.

A missionary meeting was held at the Boys School with an address by Canon Curran from Niagara, North America.

Newick Park mansion

FEBRUARY 1898

The Girls Friendly Society had a sale of work at the Reading Room.

The Parish Council meeting at the Boys School considered the new basis or standard for the County rate. The bye-laws for Newick Green were discussed.

The adults of the church choir had their supper at the Rectory.

The Cricket Club annual general meeting at the Boys School Room elected Rev F S Sclater as president. F Gravely was re-elected captain.

MARCH 1898

The Chailey Union is dissolved and is now part of the Lewes Union.

The Parish Council members have been elected – J Oldaker (schoolmaster), Aaron Martin (labourer), Mark V Wood (carrier), T Chrismas (wheelwright), Kemp Brooks (labourer), Christopher King (labourer), J Scott (platelayer), Tom Freeland (grocer) and R A Ravenhill (gentleman).

APRIL 1898

The cricket club purchased an iron roller from Jim Croucher for £5 15s.

Members of the Ladies Social Club held a dance in the Reading Room.

MAY 1898

The Rev F Sclater has drawn the attention of Chailey Rural District Council to the poor state of the road through Newick.

Newick beat Chailey at quoits on The Green.

The Parish Council discussed the question of reviving the annual Cottage Garden Show. It was also agreed to approach the London Brighton and South Coast Railway Company to achieve a better railway service in the winter. Complaints about nuisances on The Green were also raised.

PC Crouch apprehended William Pagden for driving his cart without a light. He was fined 3s 6d by Lewes Petty Sessions.

JUNE 1898

The Newick Old Benefit Society and the Newick Independent United Friends Club had their annual parade through the village together with a church service and then a dinner in a marquee at the rear of the Bull Inn.

Fletching beat Newick at quoits on The Green.

JULY 1898

At last, the pump on The Green has finally been erected despite all the lengthy complications of village rights, water rights, vested rights etc. The inauguration ceremony was performed by Mrs Clement Powell, wife of the rector, and attended by other dignitaries including those responsible for its erection. A photograph was taken. The pump was designed by Percy Gravely and beautifully completed in stone by C F Bridgman of Lewes. The metal spout, cast by J Every at the Phoenix Ironworks in Lewes represents a lion's head and the pump handle is like a lion's tail. Arthur and Tom Wood dug the well and E H and R Fuller supplied the internal machinery. The pump commemorates Queen Victoria's reign of 60 years and would have been completed for

The inauguration ceremony for the village pump on The Green – July 1898

165

the Jubilee celebrations last year but has been delayed somewhat. The pump will greatly benefit many of the villagers who, in dry weather, have to resort to an open dip spring at one corner of The Green.

The Parish Council meeting discussed footpaths.

AUGUST 1898

Thomas Horscroft was fined three shillings at Lewes Petty Sessions for neglecting to send his child to Newick School.

James Perring was fined 2s 6d for breach of the dog muzzling order.

The estate of James Robert Charles Sclater, who died in December last year, was valued at £84,139.

Vincent Wood was fined 2s 6d for delivering a quantity of coal without the necessary ticket under the Weights and Measures Act. Henry Manners who delivered the coal was fined 13s for not carrying a weighing machine.

SEPTEMBER 1898

A horticultural and agricultural show was held in the hospital field courtesy of Mr T Baden Powell. It was a great success and well attended with some fine displays in the marquee. Prizewinners included F Bannister, J Brown, G H Chrismas, W G Day, T Evans, J Mainwood, H Martin, W Martin, H Simmons, J Smith, S Smith, A Tidy, G Watts and M V Wood. The Lewes Town Band enlivened the show and sports were also held including a sack race, high jump, slow bicycle race, egg and spoon race etc. The success of the show has resulted in talk of creating a Newick or a Newick and Chailey Horticultural Society.

Thomas Williams of no fixed abode was apprehended by PC Stevens for being drunk and disorderly and was fined 10s by Lewes Police Court or, in default of payment, 7 days hard labour.

The end of season cricket match was held between the marrieds and the singles followed by supper. T Chrismas had the best batting average for the season.

Mary Ann Farley's young son aged only 4 months died.

Schoolchildren at the National School with Miss Rose Wood 1898

OCTOBER 1898

The Friendly Societies of Newick and Chailey held their annual parade with processions, the Ardingly Brass Band and a church service.

Chailey Rural District Council discussed the drainage provisions for the village where connections are now being made to the sewer.

F Homewood was fined 15s at Lewes magistrates court for being drunk in Newick.

The Parish Council discussed the issue of allotments, water supply for the village, the need for late trains on particular occasions (pantomime trains), and that the District Council ought to be informed of the defective state of the road opposite the wheelwrights shop.

The annual Sunday School treat was held with tea, crackers, prizes for attendance and proficiency, presents and concluding with God Save The Queen.

Parish Council members inspected some sites near Goldbridge to consider the practicalities of providing a bathing place and a dam.

A concert in aid of the football club was packed despite the dark, wet night.

NOVEMBER 1898

The Bonfire Boys provided the Guy Fawkes celebrations in customary manner with a procession from the Royal Oak to the principle residences. A huge bonfire was lit with effigies of the Pope and Guy being burnt. This was followed by another procession with the event finishing just before midnight.

Newick beat Fletching at whist in the Reading Room and later the 'marrieds' beat the 'singles'.

Arthur King was fined 5s at Lewes Petty Sessions for having the name on his cart drawn on with chalk instead of being painted on.

The Bonfire Boys had their annual supper at the Royal Oak with a meal, toasts and music.

The locomomotive 'Newick' built at Brighton in 1898

A locomotive built at Brighton for the London Brighton and South Coast Railway Company has been given the name of 'Newick'.

A concert at the Reading Room has raised funds for permanently fencing the cricket ground.

The Parish Council is asking the London Brighton and South Coast Railway Company to run a late train on Thursday nights from Brighton, through Newick to East Grinstead.

DECEMBER 1898

The general manager of the London Brighton and South Coast Railway Company has agreed to the request by the Newick Parish Council and the Barcombe Parish Council for a weekly late train from Brighton and Lewes. The train will operate on Thursday evenings and arrive at Newick and Chailey station at 11.39 p.m.

The Parish Council is to investigate the reason for the large increase in the poor rate made last May.

A whist match was held between the Ladies Social Club and members of the Reading Room and also between Newick and Chailey.

Frank Grover was fined £1 at Lewes Petty Sessions for assaulting Timothy Watson in November.

A meeting at the Boys School decided to form a new, properly organised Horticultural Society for Newick, the original once flourishing Society formed in the 1830's having now been defunct for several years. The purpose of the Society will be to educate the public in the growth of flowers, fruit and vegetables. A show will be held every August. Officers were elected including the Rev F S Sclater as president and Mr Hare as secretary and treasurer.

The Football Club held its annual general meeting at the Reading Room. The balance shows a deficit of 15s 10d. Officers and the committee were elected.

Lewes Petty Sessions heard the case against Sier Markwick junior who had assaulted PC Stevens and been drunk in charge of a horse and cart. Charles Croucher, the local blacksmith, gave evidence. The accused was fined 20s for drunkenness and 14 days prison for assault.

JANUARY 1899

The Ladies Social Club lost to Newick Reading Room at whist.

The annual Parish Council meeting was held presided over by R A Ravenhill.

The Newick Cricket Club held its annual general meeting at the Bull Inn and elected its officers. The Committee agreed to enclose the 3½ acre cricket ground with iron railings to accord with the requirements of the current lease. Messrs Hill and Smith's bill for the railings is £4 12s 3d with Mr Croucher charging £6 10s for labour.

The amount to be allocated to the Cottage Hospital from last year's missionary boxes and church collections will be £9 3s 8d.

The Brighton Foot Beagles met at Goldbridge and had one of the best days of the season chasing the hare.

The Ladies Social Club held a dance in the Reading Room with music by W Bates and Miss A Pickett.

FEBRUARY 1899

Newick lost to Nutley at whist but beat Barcombe and St Michael's (Lewes).

The annual report of the Cottage Hospital shows that 32 patients were treated over the year, the largest number recorded since the hospital opened in 1869. Improved sanitary systems have now been provided and connection to the main sewer. Rooms have been cleaned, distempered and papered throughout.

The adult members of the church choir had their annual supper at the Rectory courtesy of the rector and Mrs Powell.

The Parish Council meeting at the Boys School discussed the condition of footpaths, drainage, whether a fire engine was needed for the Parish etc. The possible provision of a dam on the River Ouse to create a bathing place is not to be pursued because of the expense.

The Newick Horticultural Society created last December has started enrolling members. The Society held its first 'educational' meeting with 30 members listening to a talk on onions.

*Newick Park mansion with Elisabeth Sclater in the carriage
and the horses Gladstone and Salisbury*

MARCH 1899

At the Parish Meeting 9 members were elected to the Parish Council: A Martin (gardener), J Oldaker (teacher), G H Chrismas (wheelwright), K E Brooks (mason), C W King (husbandman), M V Wood (carrier/coal merchant), J Scott (platelayer), R A Ravenhill (gentleman) and T W Freeland (grocer).

Newick beat Fletching at whist.

The Newick Horticultural Society met at the Boys School Room for a talk by Mr Chisholm, the head gardener at Beechlands, on potato growing.

A Parish meeting was held at the Boys school. W Martin, R Fuller and M V Wood were appointed as assessors and collectors of income tax, land tax and inhabited house duty.

The London Brighton and South Coast Railway Company are saying that the late train on Thursday evenings had a fair trial but was not proving remunerative – the average number of passengers being only about 11 or 12. The Parish Council still intend to urge the Railway Company to continue the late train service next winter on Saturday evenings.

APRIL 1899

The annual Easter vestry meeting at the Rectory classroom elected the church wardens and sidesmen.

The Parish Council meeting provided a summary of the Council's work over the year.

A complimentary dance was held in the Reading Room with dancing until 3 o'clock in the morning to W Bates' band.

A concert was held in the Reading Room with vocal and instrumental music.

MAY 1899

The Parish Council meetings have appointed a Committee to consider the management and working of the sewage system. Committees have also been agreed for General Purposes, Footpaths, Village Green, Technical and Secondary Education, Parish documents and Train Services.

Hector Reed took over from Eli Hollingdale as stationmaster.

An auction of Woodbine Farm with 9 acres and two new houses and buildings, for the trustees of the late W Nicholas, failed to reach its reserved price.

Thomas Horscroft, the butcher, was fined 15s plus 16s costs at Lewes Petty Sessions for having an inaccurate and unstamped scale on his barrow.

JUNE 1899

F S Sclater and his Norwegian bride were 'at home' for their tenants and employees providing a fine meal followed by cricket, stoolball, entertainment from a conjurer and ventriloquist, tea and dancing to the Chailey Industrial Band. The whole party was photographed.

1899 Payments	£	s	d
Jan 14th Charles Dawson for half cost of Lease	1	12	6
Cricket Ground Enclosure: Concert Expenses	1	14	.
" " : Croucher for labour	6	10	.
" " : Mess.rs Hill & Smith	34	12	3
May 4th Farncombe & Co		13	6
10th Newhaven Match : Railway Tickets		15	1
" " " : Luncheons		7	6
17th "The Rocks" Match : Man on ground (labour)		3	.
" " " : Luncheons		7	6
22nd Eastbourne College Match: Railway Tickets	1	16	5
" " " : Bags		4	.
" " " : Tea		10	.
31st Bedales Match: Stabling & feed for horse		1	.
June 7th Forest Row Match: Luncheons		7	6
" " " Umpires		2	.
" " Scorers		3	.
14th The Rocks match : Scorer's lunch, & fee 1/-		4	.
" " Umpires " "		4	.
17th The Hooke match : Scorer's fee		1	.
" " Carriage of Tackle repaid to Hemsley			9
24th Newhaven match : Umpire's lunch 2/6 fee 1/-		3	6
" " " : Scorers " 2/6 " 1/-		3	6
	£50	16	-

Extract from cricket club accounts 1899

A concert was held at the Reading Room with piano solos, comic songs and readings. The performers, all from Newick, were Miss Lechmere, J Weston, F Smith, Mrs Rogers, F S Sclater, Miss R Wood and Mr Francis. The proceeds will help towards purchasing gymnastic apparatus for the Boys School.

The Parish Council meeting at the Boys School discussed drainage, postal services, train timetables, overhanging trees, charges for the Reading Room etc.

JULY 1899

80 members of the Brighton Angling Association came to Newick in landaus for their annual outing and had lunch, sports, walks and dinner in brilliant weather.

Sydney Stevenson was fined 3s at Lewes Petty Sessions for allowing 3 ponies to stray on to the highway.

About 50 members of the Lewes Cyclist Club had a cycle run to the Kings Head Chailey and then on to the Bull Inn for a strawberry tea in a marquee. Cricket and baseball followed and then a one hour ride back to Lewes.

The annual dinner was held at the Bull Inn for the Newick Independent United Friends Club and the Newick Old Benefit Society. A procession marched to the church with the Ardingly Brass Band. A sermon was given by Rev Clement Powell. This was followed by a fete.

The Parish Council meeting discussed drains and trains.

A potential accident was avoided when Mr Wood's large two-horse brake travelling down the hill towards Goldbridge, carrying the band of the Chailey Industrial School, had trouble with a wobbly wheel. It was noticed just in time. The wheelwright from Newick patched it up enabling it to continue to Uckfield.

AUGUST 1899

The first flower show held under the auspices of the revived Newick Horticultural Society was held in the Cottage Hospital field with an immense, 120 foot long marquee. Some fine displays were provided by J Hickson (gardener to F S Sclater of Newick Park), Mr Chisholm (gardener to Captain Harcourt-Rose), E Richards (gardener to Rev C Powell from the Rectory), G Hodge (gardener to J D Powell of High Hurst), and many others with a total of about 400 entries. The Aeolian Glee Singers provided entertainment at the afternoon tea and the Chailey Industrial School Band and Mr W Bates String Band also played for evening dancing. The Member of Parliament Sir Henry Fletcher, always popular at Newick, attended. The event was a grand success despite the unfavourable wet weather.

NEWICK FLOWER SHOW.

This annual show, held in the hospital fie.'d by kind permission of Mr. T. Baden Powell, on Thursday, was a grand success. The entries numbered upwards of 400, and the quality of the exhibits left nothing to be desired. The general arrangements were excellent and reflect the highest credit upon the Executive Committee, which was constituted as follows :—Messrs. J. Brown, W. Chisholm, G. Dicker, J. Hickson, A. Martin, W. Martin, J. Oldaker, T. Baden Powell, E. Richards, J. Smith, S. Streeter, and J. Weston. M. Hare efficiently and courteously discharged the duties of hon. secretary. The non-competitive exhibits were very fine and greatly enhanced the beauty of the show. Amongst the exhibits worthy of special mention were those of Mr. J. Hickson, gardener to the Rev. F. S. Sclater, of Newick Park; Mr. Obisholm, gardener to Captain Harcourt Rose, of Beechlands, Newick; Mr. E. Richards, gardener to the Rev. O. Powell, Newick Rectory; Mr. G. Hodge, gardener to Mr. J. L. Powell, of Highhurst; Mr. A. Martin, Newick; Mr. John Charlton, Tunbridge Wells; Mrs. Turner, Mr. G. W. Piper, Uckfield; Messrs. Kenward and Son, Lewes; and Mr. J. Dennett, of Piltdown. The judges, who gave every satisfaction in the discharge of their onerous duties, were : Mr. A. Findlay, head gardener to Count Munster, Maresfield Park; Mr. J. Davis, head gardener to Major Thurlow, Buckham Hill House, Uckfield; and Mr. Fitt, head gardener at Oldlands, Uckfield. In many of the classes the competition was keen, and the judges had some little difficulty in deciding, but their awards were generally satisfactory. The display by cottagers was a grand one, Mr. J. Brown's tray of vegetables being almost perfect, a remark also applicable to the fine potatoes which were shown by J Cha'field. The runner and dwarf beans shown by W. Turner and John Chatfield were also good. The tray of fruit by W. Martin was a fine lot, and the same exhibitor showed some capital cooking and dessert apples. The competition for "professionals" produced some choice entries in vegetables by Mr. J. Weston, and in fruit Mr. Watts had a grand display. Apart from the distinctly horticultural side of the Newick Flower Show, the social aspect was largely in evidence, despite the somewhat unfavourable weather. There was a large and fashionable company present, and Sir Henry Fletcher, Bart., M.P. (always popular at Newick), was also present. An excellent programme of vocal and instrumental music was carried out with highly gratifying results. There were the Æolian Glee Singers, Messrs. P. Topbill, N. Richards, G. Welling, and A. Galloway, and the excellent band of the Chailey Industrial School. There was also a promenade concert, at which Miss Edith Welling sang, and dancing also was indulged in to the strains of Mr. W. Bates's String Band.

THE LIST OF AWARDS

will be found appended :—

UNDER-GARDENERS.—T. Hodges, 1st collection of vegetables, plants in pots. F. Brooker, 1st cut flowers,

2nd plants in pots.

AMATEURS AND MARKET GARDENERS.—M. Humphrey, 1st carrots, spring onions, tomatoes, 2nd celery. James Smith, 1st runner beans, celery, cucumbers, 2nd spring onions, tomatoes. G. Staplehurst, 2nd carrots, 3rd spring onions, runner beans. H. Simmonds, 2nd runner beans, 3rd celery tomatoes.

PROFESSIONALS.—J. Weston, 1st collection of vegetables, collection of annuals, 2nd cut flowers. G. W. Watts, 1st collection of fruit, 2nd collection of annuals. J. Dennett and Sons, 1st roses. O. Hatcher, 2nd collection of vegetables, roses. A. Chatfield, 2nd collection of fruit, 3rd collection of vegetables, collection of annuals, roses.

COTTAGERS.—J. Brown, 1st tray of vegetables, turnips, red cabbages, collection of wild flowers, 1st allotments, 2nd potatoes (kidney), dwarf beans. J. Chatfield, 1st potatoes (kidney), potatoes (round), autumn onions, dwarf beans, African marigolds, herbs, roses, asters, bouquet of garden flowers, plants in pots, 2nd red cabbages, carrots, 3rd tray vegetables, tomatoes, collection of wild flowers, cultivated garden. R. Grover, 1st spring onions, leeks, carrots, eschalots, pears (dessert), 2nd parsnips, beetroot, celery, apples (dessert), cultivated garden, 3rd potatoes (round). W. Turner, 1st runner beans, parsnips, celery, 2nd autumn onions, tomatoes, 3rd spring onions, pears (dessert), plums (dessert). D. Smith, 2nd for tray of fruit, damsons. J. Smith, 1st cabbages, 2nd turnips, 3rd ridge cucumbers, allotments. J. Holmes, 1st peas, 3rd apples (cooking). W. Smith, 1st marrows, damsons, 3rd stewing pears. C. Martin, 1st ridge cucumbers, 2nd round potatoes, runner beans. G. Homewood, 1st beetroots, 2nd leeks, 3rd kidney potatoes, parsnips. J. Wood, 1st tomatoes. J. Mainwood, 2nd red currants, stocks, 3rd turnips, asters, plants in pots. W. Martin, 1st tray of fruit, dessert apples, dessert apples, cooking plums, stocks, cultivated garden, 2nd cabbages, herbs, cooking plums, asters, African marigolds, plants in pots, allotments, 3rd autumn onions, turnips eschalots. lettuce dessert apples, red currants. J. Martin 1st dessert plums. J. Marchant, 1st red currants, 3rd beet. C. Martin, 1st collection wild flowers (under 14), 2nd apples (cooking), 3rd dwarf beans, marrows, bouquet garden flowers. D. Moore, 2nd ridge cucumbers. J. Wheatland, jun., 2nd eschalots, 3rd carrots. Miss E. Parris (Fort Hill), 2nd plums (dessert), 3rd damsons. C. Smith, 2nd bouquet of garden flowers, 3rd runner beans. Fanny Dicker, 2nd collection of wild flowers. Mabel Chatfield, 2nd collection wild flowers (under 14). J. Brown, 3rd leeks.

BEES AND HONEY.—C. Martin, 1st comb honey in skep, 2nd 1lb. jars of honey. J. Holmes, 1st glazed section. M. Humphrey, 1st 6lb. jars of honey. A. J. Ridley, 1st display of honey in trophy form, hive, shewing queen and working bees. J. Dennett and Sons, 1st six 1lb. sections of run honey. J. Mitchell, 2nd comb honey in skep. G. W. Watts, 2nd 1lb. glazed section, 2nd display of honey in trophy form. M. Jenner, 2nd six 1lb. sections of run honey. O. T. Overton (Crawley), 2nd hive, shewing queen and work'ng bees.

Newspaper cutting on the Newick Horticultural Society Flower Show 1899

The church choir had an outing to the Greater Britain Exhibition at Earls Court in London.

The Friendly Societies of Newick and Chailey had their annual parade and church service. They marched to the church from The Green via Cinder Hill and Roeheath.

SEPTEMBER 1899

David Smith, 50 years old and known as 'the lion tamer' and having family in Newick, accidentally drowned in the River Ouse at Lewes, supposedly the unwelcome outcome of a bet.

The cricket club held its wind-up match for the season with the 'marrieds' against the 'singles' followed by supper at the Bull Inn with toasts, songs and a summary of the year. E J Markwick heads the batting averages and E Richards is the top bowler. Members were particularly thanked for the special donations given this year towards payment for fencing of the ground. The club secretary advised the purchase of a winged, compartmented practice net to enable three or more batsmen to practise simultaneously. The Rev Lechmere spoke of the value of cricket in enabling all classes to mingle together as a community in these days when so many things tend to separate class from class.

The prizegiving for last month's flower show was held at the Boys School. Prizewinners were members of the Martin family, the Smith families, J Dennett and Sons, F Brooker, J Brown, A and J Chatfield, G Dicker, R Grover, C Hatcher, T Hodges, J Holmes, G Homewood, M Humphrey, M Jenner, J Mainwood, J Marchant, J Mitchell, W Moore, Mrs Parris, A Ridley, H Simmons, G Staplehurst, W Turner, G Watts, J Weston, J Wheatland and J Wood. Loud cheers arose when Captain Harcourt Rose offered his grounds at Beechlands for next year's Horticultural Society show. This was where the first flower show of the old Horticultural Society was held about 70 years ago and which was the subject of an 1833 copperplate engraving by the distinguished Newick engraver James Henry Hurdis.

W G Powell emigrated to Canada with his wife so he has resigned his office of manager at the National School and as a trustee of the Cottage Hospital.

The Parish Council agreed to thank the London Brighton and South Coast Railway for consenting to run a late train from Brighton to Newick and Chailey station on Saturday nights.

OCTOBER 1899

George Salvage was fined 15s at Lewes Petty Sessions for carrying coals without having the necessary scales and weights.

The Parish Council meeting considered footpaths needing repair, particularly the paths from The Green to Newick Wood, from Ketches to High Hurst, from the Boys School to Step Gate (Beechlands), from the churchyard to Blind Lane, from Western Road past the Baptist chapel to Strawberry Gardens and the paths at Blind Lane and Lovers Walk. Also discussed was whether to restore the old water pump near the tanyard by The Green and whether to have a fire brigade under the recent legislation. The Bonfire Boys could be approached to assist.

Thomas Baden Powell's cousin Colonel Baden Powell is busy in command of the forces at Mafeking.

The Church Association held a meeting in the mission room with a lantern lecture on 'Stirring Times in English History'.

The annual meeting was held of the members of the Reading Room.

W Freeland died at the age of 66 years. He was the grocer and draper on Newick Green for the last 34 years. He was an amiable and obliging gentleman and a manager of Newick school for many years.

The Horticultural Society held its annual meeting at the Boys School. The Society now has 86 members. Captain Harcourt Rose was elected president.

NOVEMBER 1899

Guy Fawkes night was a bit foggy this year. The bonfire was sodden from recent rains so did not burn well but the processions were a success. There were fireworks coloured fire, torches, guys, sky rockets, squibs, Roman candles and a brass band improvised for the occasion by the accomplished musician Kemp Brooks.

Timothy B Watson, son of D Watson of Lane End Farm, was married to Miss Naomi B Avery, the eldest daughter of H G Avery, the landlord of the Bull Inn. Apart from the Avery and Watson families others attending included Harry Fuller, Florence and Elizabeth Fuller, George and Jane Tidy, Mr and Mrs Chisholm, Ebenezer Isard, Mrs Martin, Mr Pickett, John Weston and Nell Humphries. The couple honeymooned in Hastings.

Wedding of T B Watson and Miss N B Avery, November 1899

1. Florence Avery, 2. Unknown, 3. Maude Avery, 4. Unknown, 5. Jane Tidy, 6. John Weston, 7. Nell Humphreys, 8. Mr Pickett, 9. Unknown, 10. Unknown, 11. Unknown, 12. Elizabeth Fuller, 13. Unknown, 14. Will Watson, 15. Harry Fuller, 16. Florence Fuller, 17. Mr Chisholm, 18. Mrs Chisholm, 19. George James Tidy, 20. Gertrude Best Avery, 21. Ebenezer Isard, 22. Mrs Martin, 23. Daniel Watson, 24. Ada Watson, 25. Timothy Watson, 26. Naomi Best Avery, 27. Henry George Avery, 28. Naomi Avery, 29. Lillian Avery, 30. Jessie Avery, 31. Elsie Watson, 32. Ethel Avery

A Chrysanthemum and Fruit Show was held in the Reading Room under the auspices of the Newick Horticultural Society. A floral concert was also included in the afternoon and another concert in the evening. It was all a great success with particular thanks to P H Hare the secretary of the Society.

The annual rent audit of the tenants of the Beechlands estate was held at the Crown Inn.

A lecture was given by Captain Harcourt Rose on the war currently raging in South Africa.

The Parish Council is intending to ask the post master general to install a letter box at Cornwells Bank. The Council would also like to see special railway excursion fares for villagers attending Brighton United Football Club games. No steps are to be taken to abolish the annual fair on The Green as most of the villagers oppose it being stopped.

Newick Bonfire Boys had their annual supper at their headquarters, the Royal Oak public house. The room was decorated with banners and flags. The balance sheet was read followed by toasts, music, singing, fireworks and the National Anthem.

The Ladies Social Club played The Reading Room at whist.

John Oldaker, the headmaster at the National School, is becoming increasingly concerned regarding the number of absentees. Over the last five weeks alone pupils have stayed away from school for potato picking, cover beating, picking up acorns and chestnuts, being wanted at home or otherwise employed. Newick School Board will be requested to enforce the law by taking action against the offenders.

DECEMBER 1899

A well attended meeting was held at the Boys School to discuss the steps to be taken to assist the Boer War Distress Fund. It was agreed to have a house-to-house collection throughout the Parish.

The Cricket Club held its annual meeting at the Bull Inn.

The Royal Oak Slate Club held its annual supper. 18s 3d was raised for the War Fund. The secretary, T Smith, said that although a great many people were averse to these clubs they were very useful, especially to men too old to join the larger friendly societies.

GOD SAVE THE QUEEN

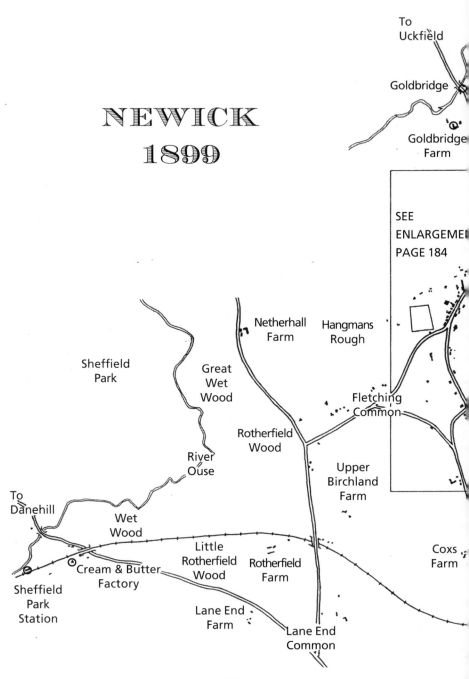

NEWICK
1899

To
Uckfield

Goldbridge

Goldbridge
Farm

SEE
ENLARGEMEN
PAGE 184

Netherhall
Farm

Hangmans
Rough

Sheffield
Park

Great
Wet
Wood

Fletching
Common

Rotherfield
Wood

River
Ouse

Upper
Birchland
Farm

To
Danehill

Wet
Wood

Little
Rotherfield
Wood

Rotherfield
Farm

Coxs
Farm

Cream & Butter
Factory

Sheffield
Park
Station

Lane End
Farm

Lane End
Common

182

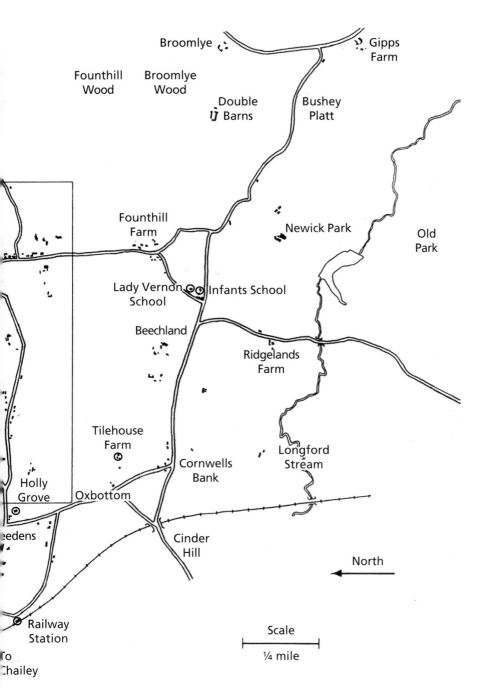

Broomlye

Gipps
Farm

Founthill
Wood

Broomlye
Wood

Double
Barns

Bushey
Platt

Founthill
Farm

Newick Park

Old
Park

Lady Vernon
School

Infants School

Beechland

Ridgelands
Farm

Tilehouse
Farm

Longford
Stream

Holly
Grove

Cornwells
Bank

Oxbottom

eedens

Cinder
Hill

North

Railway
Station

Scale

¼ mile

To
Chailey

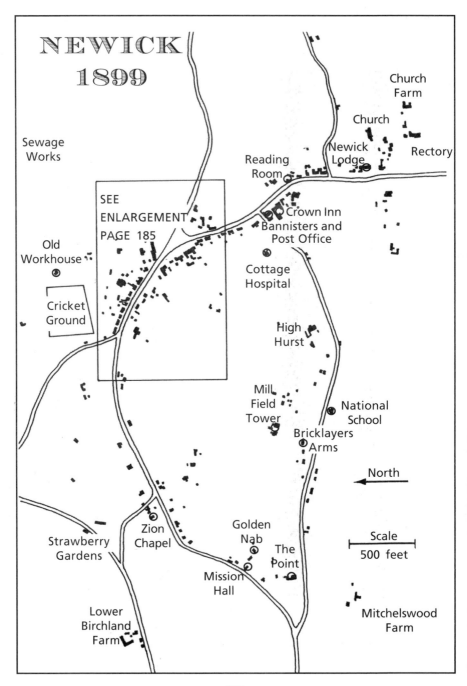

NEWICK
1899

Sewage
Works

Church
Farm

Church

Reading
Room

Newick
Lodge

Rectory

SEE
ENLARGEMENT
PAGE 185

Crown Inn
Bannisters and
Post Office

Old
Workhouse

Cottage
Hospital

Cricket
Ground

High
Hurst

Mill
Field
Tower

National
School

Bricklayers
Arms

North

Zion
Chapel

Golden
Nab

Strawberry
Gardens

The
Point

Scale
500 feet

Mission
Hall

Lower
Birchland
Farm

Mitchelswood
Farm

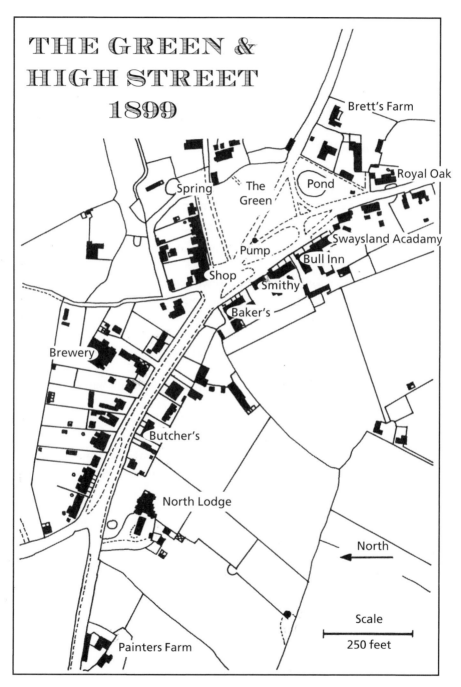

THE GREEN &
HIGH STREET
1899

Brett's Farm

Royal Oak

Spring

The
Green

Pond

Swaysland Acadamy

Pump

Bull Inn

Shop

Smithy

Baker's

Brewery

Butcher's

North Lodge

North

Scale

250 feet

Painters Farm

A Chronology
of Some of the Events in the Village

Just prior to the period of the diary the Cottage Hospital had been built in 1869 and the National School had opened in 1874

1875 School Board created for the Parish.

1876 Railway line proposed through Newick and Chailey.

1877 Scarlet fever epidemic.

1878 Contract for building the railway finalised.

1879 Building of the railway line commenced. Railway Reading Room provided.

1880 Work continued on building the railway.

1881 National Census held. John Oldaker took charge of National School.

1882 Railway station opened. Infants school built next to Lady Vernon School.

1883 The first accident on the new railway line.

1884 New cricket club founded.

1885 Cricket club started playing at Mitchelswood ground.

1886 Newick Choral Society created. Newick branch of the Primrose League formed.

1887 Enlargement of the church was completed. Newick Football Club formed. Queen Victoria's Silver Jubilee celebrations.

1888 Parts of the village provided with decent drainage.

1889 New organ and lectern installed in the church.

1890 A Men's Guild and a Mothers' Guild were established.

1891 National Census held. Provision of a new Reading Room discussed.

1892 Cricket Club started playing at the Home Field. Reading Room and the Mission hall built.

1893 Village celebrations for Duke of York's wedding.

1894 Churchyard extended.

1895 Parish Council established. Cricket club moved to Workhouse field.

1896 Parish Council was appointed to look after The Green. Newick Liberal and Radical Association founded.

1897 Queen Victoria's Diamond Jubilee celebrations. James Henry Sclater died.

1898 Newick Horticultural Society re-established. Pump erected on The Green. Better drainage provided for the village.

1899 The first flower show under the auspices of the re-established Newick Horticultural Society.

BIBLIOGRAPHY AND SOURCES

As stated at the beginning of this book most of the information for the diary has been taken from the contemporary Sussex newspapers for 1875-1899. Also, information can be gleaned from a variety of sources including the following:

Selected post-1899 Sussex newspapers contain various articles, obituaries etc including a full description of the church in the Sussex Express for 22.6.34 and 29.6.34.

Books, magazines etc

J Lindsey 'The Story of a Sussex Village' (1983)

'Victoria County History of Sussex' Volume 7 (1940)

Kellys Directories 1878-1899

National Census 1881 and 1891

Ordnance Survey maps

Newick Parish Council 'Newick A Pictorial History' (1991)

D Arscott 'Tales From The Parish Pump' (1994)

'Newick Cricket Club 1884-1984 A Centenary Celebration' (1984)

Newick Parish Council 'Newick Village Week 2nd to 10th July 1994' Souvenir Programme (1994)

County Age Concern 'Sussex in the Old Days' (1987)

Tessa Harvey 'The Sclaters – History of a Sussex Family' (1994)

Gordon Diamond and J P Baker 'History and Guide' (to the church) (1958 and later revisions)

Beryl Jones and Joyce Lindsey 'Newick Church and its People Through The Ages' (1981)

Sussex County Magazine July 1948 and September 1930

'Sussex Life' magazine September 1979

Edna and Mac McCarthy 'Sussex River Upstream from Lewes to the Sources' (1979)

Railway Magazine (October 1954 and April 1962)

Bluebell News (October 1960)

Bluebell Railway Preservation Society 'The Handbook of the Bluebell Line' (1962)

Terry Cole 'Bluebell Railway – Steaming On' (1970)

Klaus Marx 'Bluebell Line Historical Album 1879-1965' (1978)

Michael S Welch 'Rails To Sheffield Park' (1988)

The East Sussex Record Office in Lewes includes the following:

Parish Register transcripts – births, marriages and deaths.

Newick Parish Magazines 1886-1894, 1898 and 1899 (PAR 428 7/6/1, 2 and 3)

Vestry minutes (PAR 428 14/2/1)

Parish Council Committees

    General Purposes Committee 1897 (P 428/2/1)

    Pump Committee (P 428/2/2)

    Allotments Committee 1891 (P 428/2/3)

Plan of Newick Green to show site of proposed pump (1894?) (P 428 10/3)

School Documents

    Infants School Log Book 1882-1925 (ESC 124 2/1 and 2)

    Conveyance for National School (PAR 428 25/1)

    National School Log Book 1875-1923 (ESC 124 3/1)

    School Board Minutes 1878-1903 (C/E11/30-32)

Chailey Rural Sanitary Authority minutes (RCH/TR 1/1, 2, 3)

Archives of the Oldaker family (AMS 5785)

Thomas Baden Powell papers 1864-1942

    Volume II (AMS 5785/11)

    Volume III (AMS 5785/12)

Victoria Diamond Jubilee   (AMS 5785/20 and P 428 10/4)

Photographs various   (AMS 5785/9/2)

(AMS 5785/9/3)

(AMS 5785/17/1 and 2)

(AMS 5785/18/2)

December 1894 request to attend the first Parish Council meeting (P 428 10/1)

Lord of the Manor appoints Parish Council as deputy for village green (1896) (P 428 10/2)

Pump on village green – details of plaque and base (1897) (P 428 10/5)

Rate of assessment for discharging instalment due on money for building wall around churchyard (P 428 11/1)

Poor rate book 1879-1880(P 428 11/2)

Enlargement of church 1886   (PAR 428 4/1/1)

Churchwardens Accounts 1891-1917 (PAR 428 9/2/1)

Lease of workhouse field for cricket and sports (SRL/5/3)

Register of licenses 1872-1890 (PTS 1/3/1 and 2)

Map of proposed railway by engineer J Wolfe Barry (QDP 428)

Stopping up of public footpath near railway station 1884 (QDP 485)

The Public Record Office at Kew includes the following:

Correspondence, reports and information on schools and the School Board (ED 2/434, ED 6/67, ED 7/121, ED 21/17280, ED 21/17281, ED 49/7593.

Valuation Office records created under the Finance (1909-1910) Act. Although outside the 1875-1899 period these records assist in identifying properties etc (IR 58/12810, 12811, 12812, 12813, 12814 and 12815. IR 124/1/104 and 105).

Agricultural Returns for the Parish   (MAF 68/889 etc)

Chailey Union correspondence, annual reports etc (MH 12/12808, 12809, 12810, 12811 and 12812)

Railway records – letters, minutes, contracts, staff registers and reports (RAIL 414/3 – RAIL 414/779. RAIL 1110/288. MT 29/43).

The Sussex Archaeological Society library includes the following:

A collection of papers and notebooks of F Bentham-Stevens

Memories of Old Newick by a Sussex Woman (Ellen Fuller)

INDEX

The figures refer to the month/year

Basketmakers Arms, 7/91

Bates, 1/76, 9/76, 6/84, 5/85 (including photograph), 9/86, 1/87, 3/91, (including photograph) 3/93, 1/99, 4/99, 8/99 (and in 1893 cricket team photograph and 1894 football team photograph)

Bathing facility, 1/98, 10/98, 2/99

Bayliss, 4/84, 8/87, 11/93

Beechland, Beechlands, 11/77, 8/78, 12/78, 3/79, 11/79, 8/81, 8/82, 8/83, 11/83, 8/84, 9/85, 8/88, 11/88, 4/89, 8/90, 11/90, 7/91, 8/91, 8/92, 11/92, 4/95, 7/95, 11/96, 2/97, 11/97, 3/99, 9/99, 10/99, 11/99.

Beef (free distribution at Christmas), 12/90, 12/93

Bell ringing, 11/80, 1/83, 12/85, 6/87, 1/92, 6/93, 1/96, 6/97

Bennett, 7/78

Bertram, 5/97

Best, 5/83, 7/95, 11/99 (including photograph)

Bicycles, 3/93

Bigge, 11/97

Birchland, 2/75, 11/90

Blaauw, 9/76, 2/77, 8/78, 12/78, 10/79, 12/79 (including photograph), 6/81, 8/81, 3/82, 8/83, 3/84, 8/84, 5/87, 4/89, 5/89, 11/89, 8/90, 11/90, 7/91, 8/92, 9/93, 9/95, 11/97

Blencowe, 6/75, 6/81, 2/87

Blind Lane, 10/96, 10/99

Board of Trade, 11/78, 7/82, 10/82

Boer War Distress Fund, 12/99

Bonfire Boys, 11/77, 11/84, 11/85, 11/86, 11/89, 11/93, 6/97, 11/98, 10/99, 11/99

Bonfire Celebrations (Guy Fawkes night), 11/76, 11/77, 11/78, 11/79, 11/83, 11/84, 11/86, 11/87, 11/88, 11/89, 11/90, 11/91, 11/92, 11/93, 11/94, 11/95, 11/96, 11/97, 11/98, 11/99

Bonfire Society, 11/87, 10/88, 11/88, 9/90, 11/91, 11/92, 11/94, 11/96, 11/97

Booker, 11/77, 10/89, 9/94, 9/86

Bowden, 3/76

Boxall, 11/83

Brand, 10/97

Boxall, 11/83

Bretts Farm, 9/86, 2/88, 9/91, 4/92, 10/92, 1/94, 10/94

Brewery, 8/79, 1/87, 4/89, 8/91, 9/92 (plan), 6/95, 9/95, 3/96

Bricklayers Arms, 8/80, 11/80, 6/81, 11/81, 11/86, 11/90, 11/91, 11/92, 3/93

Bridgman, 7/98

Brighton,

All Souls Sunday School, 6/94

Angling Association, 7/99

Anscombe Brass Band, 9/75, 9/76, 7/78

Arms, 4/95

Bostel Brothers, 7/88

Bryan and Son, 7/91

Corporation and Guardians, 7/84

Davis, Messrs,

District Church Teachers Association, 9/93

Dutton and Thorowgood, 8/97

First Sussex Artillery Volunteers, 8/95

Foot Beagles, 12/96, 1/99

Greyhound, The, 7/88

Hanningtons, 7/88

Holy Trinity Church, 7/86, 7/88

Lynn and Sons, 7/88

Pantechnicon, 8/84

Pike and Co., 7/78

Railway Works, 7/84

Reed and Son, 7/85

Robins and Son, 8/88

Saint Johns Fife and Drum Band, 5/94

Snowdrops, 5/79, 2/84

Swimming Club, 9/92

Town Band, 11/76

Weslyn Sunday School, 7/87

Britton, 5/96

Brock, 5/93

Brook, 9/75, 9/76, 2/78, 8/79, 6/84, 10/84, 5/85 (including photograph), 11/86, 3/87, 5/87, 3/88, 6/88, 11/90

Brooke, 1/87, 3/94

Brooks, 7/75, 2/76, 11/80, 7/82, 6/84, 7/86, 9/86, 6/93, 9/94, 3/98, 3/99, 11/99 (and in 1893 cricket team photograph)

Broomlye, 2/75, 4/76, 1/94

Brown, 10/92, 9/94, 5/97, 9/98, 9/99

Buck, 9/75, 10/78, 12/79, 11/80, 12/82

Buckland, 7/77

Buckmaster, 2/90

Budgen, 11/80, 11/90, 12/94

Bullfield, 3/76

Bull Inn, 2/75, 7/75, 9/75, 2/76, 7/76, 8/76, 9/76, 2/77, 5/77, 7/77, 5/78, 7/78, 3/79, 5/79, 7/79, 12/79, 7/81, 1/82, 5/83, 12/83, 3/84, 4/84, 5/84, 6/84, 7/84, 11/84, 5/85, 7/85, 9/85, 11/85, 3/86, 5/86, 11/86, 3/87, 5/87, 7/87, 10/87, 11/87, 1/88, 4/88, 7/88, 8/88, 9/88, 10/88, 11/88, 3/89, 5/89, 7/89, 10/89, 11/89, 5/90, 7/90, 9/90, 11/90, 3/91, 4/91, 5/91, 7/91, 10/91, 11/91, 3/92, 6/92, 7/92, 10/92, 11/92, 3/93, 5/93, 9/93, 10/93, 11/93, 1/94, 5/94, 7/94, 11/94, 4/95, 5/95, 7/95, 8/95, 5/96, 7/96, 9/96, 2/97, 6/97, 10/97, 6/98, 1/99, 7/99, 9/99, 11/99, 12/99

Burstow Hunt, 1/83

Bushy Platt, 1/79, 1/82

Callaway, 1/83

Card Club (Newick and Chailey), 4/91

Carlsden, 4/95

Carr, 8/75

Carvill, 10/75, 7/89

Caws, 2/78

Census, 4/81, 4/91

Chailey

    Card Club, 4/91

    Choral Society, 11/86

    Common, 6/86, 7/95

    Cricket, 6/84

    Decanal Educational Union, 7/75

    Drum and Fife Band, 11/89

    Foresters, 10/96

    Friendly Society, 10/93, 9/94

Font, 8/87, 4/88
Harmonium, 12/89
Lectern, 5/89
Missionary Society, 10/89
Organ, 12/89, 1/90, 5/90, 12/90, 4/93, 6/95
Reredo, 4/97
Restoration/Enlargement, 1/86, 2/86, 3/86, 4/86, 5/86, 8/86, 5/87, 7/87, 8/87, 1/88, 5/88, 7/88
Road, 6/92, 7/94, 10/94, 1/95, 7/95
Wardens, 4/79, 4/87, 3/91, 4/97, 4/99
Cinder Hill, 6/80, 11/80, 8/99
Cinque Ports (Lewes) Rifles, 7/84, 7/94
Clarence, Duke of, 1/92
Coal Club, 11/83, 12/90, 1/95, 10/95
Cockfield Lane, 10/89
Coleman, 7/75, 9/83
Collector of Rates, Taxes, Duty, 3/87, 3/90, 3/91, 3/93, 3/95, 3/96, 3/97, 3/99
Collings, 9/86
Collom, 11/89
Colman, 9/94, 2/95
Colonels Bank/Cornwells Bank, 1/76, 4/77, 8/77, 11/89, 11/90, 5/95, 2/97, 11/99
Comber/Coomber, 4/76, 11/76, 12/76
Conservative Association, 9/85, 2/88, 3/89, 4/93
Constable, Special, 5/79, 12/80
Cooksbridge Fife and Drum Band, 11/88
Cookson, 6/82
Cooper, 3/94, 2/97
Coppard, 3/82
Copyholders, 10/96, 4/97
Corbett, 5/97
Cornwell, 3/97
Cornwells Bank, see Colonels Bank
Cottagers Flower Show/Garden Show, 9/75, 9/76, 9/79, 9/83, 9/84, 9/85, 9/86, 9/88, 10/88, 8/89, 9/90, 10/90, 9/91, 8/92, 9/93, 9/94, 11/94, 5/98

Cottage Hospital, 3/77, 5/77, 9/78, 10/79, 8/80, 6/81, 9/82, 1/83, 12/83, 5/84, 4/85, 12/85, 1/87, 3/87, 5/88, 3/89, 10/89, 1/90, 12/90, 3/91, 11/91, 4/92, 8/92, 12/92, 5/93, 10/93, 2/94, 2/95, 9/95, 4/97, 10/97, 1/99, 2/99, 8/99, 9/99

Cottingham, 3/87, 10/87

Cottington, 12/85

Countess Dowager of Hampden, 7/93

Countess Dowager of Roden, 7/86, 12/90, 11/97, 8/92

Cox, 10/92, 3/93

Cream and butter factory, 4/90

Cribbage, 9/93, 3/96, 2/97, 1/98

Cricket / Newick Cricket Club, 12/83, 3/84, 5/84, 6/84, 10/84, 1/85, 5/85, 9/85, 10/85, 3/86, 3/87, 10/87, 5/88, 10/88, 6/89, 10/89, 11/89, 4/90, 9/90, 5/91, 10/91, 4/92, 5/92, 10/92, 4/93, 10/93, 4/94, 5/94, 12/94, 2/95, 4/95, 5/95, 6/95, 7/95, 1/96, 2/96, 3/96, 4/96, 9/96, 2/97, 4/97, 10/97, 2/98, 11/98, 1/99, 9/99, 12/99

Cross, 12/91

Crosse, 12/93

Crouch, 5/98

Croucher, 12/98

Crown Inn, 1/75, 4/76, 1/77, 2/78, 1/79, 6/82, 7/82, 10/83, 9/85, 11/87, 7/88, 9/88, 11/88, 8/89, 11/90, 9/91, 11/92, 7/94, 9/94, 11/97, 11/99

Cuckfield Harriers/Cuckfield and Haywards Heath Harriers, 2/75, 2/76, 2/77

Curran, 1/98

Danehill, 5/85

Davis, 12/80, 7/88

Daws, 7/80

Day, 2/85, 3/92, 9/98

Deacon, 4/92, 12/92, 7/94, 4/95

Depury, 11/93, 3/94, 8/94, 3/97

Dickens, 10/78

Dicker, 9/76, 3/88, 9/99

Diocesan Inspector, 8/86

Diplock, 7/78 (and in 1894 football team photograph)

Diphtheria, 7/85, 8/93

Dobson and Son, 5/86

Dodge, 8/92, 8/93, 3/94, 8/94, 12/96

Dodson, 11/85

Dog licence, 7/89

Dog muzzling order, 8/98

Double Barns, 1/82

Douch, 7/80

Dougherty, 4/78, 10/79

Doust, 1/76, 5/77, 3/80, 3/90, 10/93, 2/94

Drainage/sewerage, 12/85, 5/88, 1/94, 3/94, 3/95, 6/95, 3/96, 1/97, 3/97, 4/97, 5/97, 6/97, 11/97, 12/97, 10/98, 2/99, 5/99, 6/99, 7/99

Drum and Fife Band (Newick), see Fife

Dumsday, 7/76, 1/83

Eastland, 11/78, 11/80

Eddis, 1/82

Education Department, 4/83

Electricity, 9/82

Elliot, 3/97

Elphick, 9/75, 7/93 (and in 1894 football team photograph)

Evangelization Society, 7/95

Evans, 11/80, 5/97, 9/98

Evening classes, 10/81, 2/82, 10/97, 11/88, 5/89

Every, 7/98

Faber, 7/80, 12/82

Fair (Newick), 5/76, 5/77, 4/79, 5/81, 5/82, 4/83, 4/84, 5/85, 4/87, 4/88, 4/90, 5/93, 4/94, 4/95, 4/96, 4/97, 11/99

Fairclough, 4/87

Fares, 2/86

Farley, 7/75, 9/98 (and in 1894 football team photograph)

Fenner, 10/80

Ferguson, 3/76

Fife and Drum Band (Newick), 11/77, 11/78, 11/95, 6/97, 9/97

Figgis, 12/92

Firbank, 11/78, 4/80

Fire engine/Fire Brigade, 2/99, 10/99

First Sussex Engineers, 5/96

Fitzhugh, 1/93

Fletcher, Sir Henry, MP, 9/91, 1/95, 2/97, 8/99

Fletching, 12/77, 9/78, 12/79, 1/83, 10/87, 3/96

    Brass Band, 4/84, 5/84, 11/85, 7/86, 11/86, 5/87, 6/87, 7/87, 7/88, 5/89, 5/90, 7/90, 11/90, 5/91, 7/91, 7/93, 10/93, 7/94, 11/94, 5/95, 7/95, 11/97

    Chess, 3/91, 10/93, 11/93, 12/93, 4/96, 12/96

    Choir, 7/93

    Choral Society, 11/86

    Common, 7/91, 7/94, 9/97

    Cricket, 7/84, 9/86

    Drum and Fife Band, 2/97

    Mill, 2/75

    Quoits, 6/98

    Reading Room, 10/93

    Whist, 4/94, 1/96, 1/97, 12/97, 11/98, 3/99

Football Club (Newick), 10/87, 5/88, 10/88, 9/89, 5/90, 3/91, 10/91, 2/92, 10/92, 4/93, 10/93, 12/93, 3/94, 10/94, 10/95, 11/95, 8/96, 10/98, 12/98

Footpaths, 11/84, 5/95, 9/95, 2/97, 7/98, 2/99, 5/99, 10/99

Fount Hill, 3/76, 5/86, 3/87, 5/89, 11/90, 2/97

Founthill Farm, 2/97, 5/97

Founthill Wood, 3/79

Francis, 1/93, 5/97, 6/99

Freeland, 8/82, 10/87, 3/88, 2/90, 3/93, 2/97, 5/97, 3/98, 3/99, 10/99

Friendly Societies – see Chailey Friendly Society, Chailey Foresters, Independent United Friends Club, Old Benefit Society, Old Friendly Society, South Saxon Lodge of Oddfellows

Fruit, 8/91

Fuller, 4/75, 9/76, 11/78, 10/80, 6/84, 6/85, 11/86, 10/88 (including photograph), 10/89, 12/89, 1/93, 3/93, 7/98, 3/99, 11/99 (including photograph) and in 1893 cricket team photograph

Funnell, 6/75, 5/87

Gartside-Tipping, 10/85

Gas, 4/97

Gaston, 3/76

Gates, 9/88
George, 1/83
Gibbins, 12/92
Gibson, 10/87
Gilbert, 7/75, 12/75, 2/76, 5/76, 7/76, 8/76, 9/76, 9/78, 8/79, 5/84, 7/84, 9/86, 1/97
Gilham, 1/88, 9/91, 12/91
Gipps/Gypps Farm, 5/82
Gipps/Gypps Wood, 1/80
Girls Friendly Society (Newick), 6/86, 8/96, 2/98
Glover, 5/85 (including photograph), 9/90, 7/92
Goddard, 7/95
Godfrey, 2/94
Goldbridge and Goldbridge Farm, 2/77, 2/78, 1/83, 7/86, 3/87, 6/88, 11/90, 12/92, 4/94, 11/95, 6/96, 7/96, 12/96, 1/97, 1/99, 7/99
Golden Cottage, 3/82
Golden Nab, 9/85
Golden Point, 10/78, 1/79
Gospel Mission, 5/90
Gower, 6/86
Grace W G, 7/83, 5/85, 5/86, 5/91, 11/91, 5/96
Grainger, in 1894 football team photograph
Gravely, 2/75, 2/77, 9/77, 10/77, 10/78, 4/79, 7/79, 9/79, 10/79, 11/79, 9/80, 2/82, 1/83, 3/83, 5/83, 10/83, 11/83, 12/83, 3/84, 6/84, 9/84, 10/84, 4/85, 5/85 (including photograph), 7/85, 1/87, 3/87, 4/87, 8/87, 1/88, 3/88, 3/89, 2/90, 5/91, 5/92, 5/96, 6/96, 7/96, 8/96, 11/97, 2/98, 7/98
Great Rotherfield Wood, 12/77
Great Wood, 3/79
Green, 6/86
Green, The,
    Bye-laws, 2/98
    Nuisances, 5/98, 11/99
    Parish Council to take over, 5/95, 9/96, 10/96, 11/96, 2/97
    Spring, 7/98
Greenway, 9/80
Grosse, 10/94, 10/95

Grover, 12/88, 11/93, 7/97, 12/98, 9/99

Gulcher Electric Light and Power Co, 9/82

Guns Wood, 1/83

Gurr, 6/82

Guy Fawkes night – see Bonfire Celebrations

Hallett, 11/97

Hammond, 4/86, 8/86 (including photograph), 11/86, 1/87, 4/89, 7/89, 8/89, 10/92

Hampton, 2/87, 3/88

Hand and Heart Club, 7/79

Hanger Wood, 2/97

Hangers, The, 4/94

Hangmans Rough, 3/79

Hangmans Wood, 2/78

Harbour, 9/76

Harcourt-Rose, 11/96, 8/99, 9/99, 10/99, 11/99

Hare, 6/97, 12/98, 11/99

Hare Hunt, 2/75, 2/76, 2/77, 2/78, 3/79, 3/80, 1/82, 3/87

Harris's Fair, 4/97

Harvest Home, 9/75, 9/76, 10/83, 10/86, 9/87, 10/88, 9/89, 10/90, 10/92, 10/93, 10/94, 10/95

Hatcher, 9/99

Hayler, 6/80

Haywards Heath,

    Asylum, 7/77, 3/87, 10/87

    Black Pearl Minstrels, 11/89

    Chess, 3/94

Heale, 6/95

Heaseman, 12/86

Hemsley, 5/82, 3/84, 6/84, 5/85 (including photograph), 10/87, 9/88, 9/93, 6/97

Henty, 7/82, 5/85 (including photograph), 5/89

Herbert, 11/81

Hickson, 8/99

High Hurst, 8/86, 11/94, 4/95, 8/99, 10/99

Hill, 9/94

Hills, 9/86

Hilton, 9/80

Hoadley, 2/77

Hobbs, 6/86, 3/93

Hodge, 8/80, 2/84, 8/99

Hodges, 1/88, 9/94, 1/95, 2/97, 5/97, 9/99 (and in 1893 cricket team
    photograph)

Hollingdale, 7/97, 5/99

Hollygrove, 11/90, 11/92, 11/94, 11/97

Holmes, 9/99

Home Farm, 3/87, 11/90

Home Field, 4/92, 5/92, 10/92, 4/93, 7/93, 10/93, 1/94, 6/94, 4/95

Homewood, 9/86, 9/94, 10/98, 9/99

Hops/Hop picking, 4/76, 9/77, 6/79, 7/83, 10/83, 9/88, 9/89, 12/92

Horscraft 6/80

Horscroft, 12/80, 8/98, 5/99

Horsted Keynes, 6/95

Horticultural Society (Newick), 9/98, 12/98, 2/99, 3/99, 8/99, 9/99,
    10/99, 11/99 (also, see Cottagers Flower Show)

Hospital – see Cottage Hospital

Hoste, 8/89

Hove,

    Albion, 12/93, 3/94

    Lion Slate Club, 7/96

Howell, 6/75, 9/76, 2/77, 4/79, 7/82, 7/85, 3/87, 4/87, 10/87, 3/88,
    4/89, 3/90, 3/93, 1/94, 12/94

Hubbard, 9/85

Hughes, 11/90, 11/97

Humphrey/Humphreys, 3/84, 9/99, 11/99 (including photograph)

Hurdis, 9/99

Hydrophobia, 10/77

Illumination (lamps), 4/97

Incorporated Society for Promoting the Enlargement, Building and
    Repairing of Churches and Chapels, 4/86

Independent United Friends Club (Newick), 7/84, 7/85, 7/86, 7/87,
    7/88, 7/89, 7/90, 7/91, 11/91, 6/92, 7/93, 7/94, 9/94, 7/95,
    7/96, 10/96, 6/97, 6/98, 10/98, 7/99, 8/99

Industrial School (Chailey) – see Chailey

Ingram, 9/77, 2/87, 10/92

Inspector of Nuisances, 11/79

Isard, 8/78, 3/87, 12/94, 11/99 (including photograph) and further photograph 1896.

Ivy Lodge, 9/75

Izzard, 11/90

Jackeys Farm, 12/85

Jenner, 9/94, 9/99

Jones, 11/79, 5/81, 6/81, 10/93, 2/94

Joseph, 3/91

Journal of Horticulture and Cottage Gardener, 10/76

Jubilee (Diamond), Victoria, 4/97, 5/97, 6/97, 7/98

Jubilee (Golden), Victoria, 3/87, 4/87, 5/87, 6/87, 8/87

Keeling, 1/75, 4/76

Kennard, 2/77

Kenton, 3/89, 1/90

Kenward, 9/76, 2/79, 10/85, 12/96

Ketches, 11/84, 11/90, 12/90, 2/92, 9/95, 11/95, 10/99

King, 12/94, 3/98, 11/98, 3/99

Knight, 1/78

Kingsland, 2/90, 9/94 (and in 1893 cricket team photograph)

Knight, 1/78

Ladies Social Club, 4/96, 7/96, 5/97, 4/98, 12/98, 1/99, 11/99

Lamb public house, Piltdown, 5/97

Lambert, 10/83

Lane End Common, 1/79

Lane End Farm, 11/99

Lane H C – see Lord of the Manor

Langridge, 6/93, 7/95

Langrish, 8/75

Larkin/Larkins, 1/85, 5/85 (including photograph), 11/85, 9/86, 11/86, 6/95, 10/95, 6/96, 7/96

Laundry, 6/92, 3/96

Lazurus, 11/89

Lechmere, 6/99, 9/99

Leney, 3/95

Lewes

    Cliffe Parish, 2/96, 2/97

    Conservative Association/Club, 4/91, 9/93, 10/95, 11/97

    Cyclist Club, 5/90, 7/99

    Fire Brigade, 2/88

    Protestant Alliance, 9/90

    Reading Room, 1/98

    Saint Michael's Social Club, 2/97, 2/99

    Star Hotel, 10/76

    Union, 3/98

    Volunteer and Town Band, 7/81, 9/88, 9/98

    Working Men's Liberal Association, 6/90

Lewis, 9/79

Liberal and Radical Association (Newick), 11/96, 5/97, 10/97, 1/98

Library, 1/86, 3/88, 5/88

Lindfield, 2/92

Little Rotherfield Wood, 3/79

Local Government Inspector/Board, 12/85, 1/86, 5/97, 6/97

Locomotive 'Newick', 11/98 (including photograph)

London – visits to

    Buffalo Bill's Wild West Show, 8/87, 7/92

    Crystal Palace, 7/93

    Indian Exhibition, 8/86, 7/96

    International Fisheries Exhibition, 10/83

    International Horticultural Exhibition, 7/92

    Moore and Burgess Minstrels, 7/89

    Naval Exhibition, 7/91

    Saint James Hall, 7/89

    Saint Paul's Cathedral, 9/94

    Thames, 9/94

    Tower Bridge, 9/94

    Tower of London, 9/94

    Victorian Exhibition, 8/97

    Whitehall, 3/75

    Zoological Gardens, 7/89

Neve, 11/84, 5/85, 11/86, 3/87

Netherhall, 2/75, 2/78, 1/83

Newhaven Town Band, 9/92

Newick

    Lodge, 12/84, 11/90, 7/93, 5/94, 8/96

    Old Park, 2/80, 2/94

    Park, 6/75, 10/76, 1/79, 6/79, 11/79, 12/79, 1/80, 11/80, 12/81, 1/82, 10/83, 12/83, 8/84, 10/84, 11/84, 6/85, 10/85, 7/86, 8/86, 10/86, 3/87, 7/87, 8/87, 9/87, 7/88, 8/88, 9/88, 10/88, 11/88, 5/89, 8/89, 9/89, 10/89, 11/89, 8/90, 10/90, 11/90, 12/90, 1/91, 11/91, 8/92, 10/92, 11/92, 1/93, 8/93, 9/93, 10/93, 8/94, 11/94, 10/95, 12/96, 2/97, 12/97, 8/99

    Park Harriers, 1/82

    Wood, 2/77, 10/99

Newnham, 12/79, 12/80

Nicholas, 9/97, 5/99

Norfolk, Duchess of, 1/81

Norman, 6/76, 11/97

North Lodge, 11/81, 6/82, 7/86, 11/90, 12/90, 6/93, 11/97

Nurse, Parish, 3/89, 2/90, 12/91, 12/92

Nutley

    Chess, 1/94, 11/94, 1/96, 2/97, 12/97

    Football, 11/95

    Whist, 12/97, 1/99

Oak, Royal – see Royal

Ockenden Band, 7/76

Oddfellows, 7/75, 7/76, 7/77, 7/78, 7/81

Oldaker, 7/81, 3/84, 6/84, 10/84, 12/84, 2/85, 5/85 (including photograph), 8/86, 8/87, 10/87, 8/88, 10/88, 9/89, 10/89, 10/91, 1/92, 12/94, 3/98, 3/99, 11/99

Old Benefit Society/Friendly Society (Newick), 5/76, 5/77, 5/78, 5/79, 6/83, 5/84, 5/86, 5/87, 5/89, 8/89, 5/90, 5/91, 6/92, 5/93, 10/93, 5/94, 9/94, 5/95, 5/96, 10/96, 6/97, 6/98, 10/98, 7/99, 8/99

Osborne, 6/84, 9/86

Osbourne, 6/94

Otter, 1/94, 4/94

Ouse, River, 5/75, 11/75, 2/77, 7/77, 1/79, 6/86, 7/91, 10/91, 1/94, 4/94, 5/96, 12/96, 1/98, 10/98, 2/99, 9/99

Ouse Angling Preservation Society, 1/94

Overseers, 4/75, 4/79, 3/86, 3/87, 3/90, 7/90, 3/91, 11/91, 3/92, 3/93, 4/95

Oxbottom, 11/90, 11/97, 1/98

Packham, 1/87

Pagden, 5/98

Pages Band, 7/85, 2/86, 1/87, 12/89, 12/90, 12/91, 4/93, 12/93, 12/94, 12/95, 12/96

Painters Farm, 9/81, 4/85, 9/91, 8/94

Parish Council (Newick), 11/94, 12/94, 1/95, 3/95, 4/95, 5/95, 9/95, 10/95, 11/95, 12/95, 4/96, 9/96, 2/97, 4/97, 5/97, 9/97, 11/97, 1/98, 2/98, 3/98, 5/98, 7/98, 10/98, 11/98, 12/98, 1/99, 2/99, 3/99, 4/99, 5/99, 6/99, 7/99, 9/99, 10/99, 11/99

Parish Meeting/Vestry Meeting (Newick), 1/79, 4/79, 3/86, 3/87, 3/88, 3/89, 3/90, 3/91, 3/92, 3/93, 4/93, 4/95, 3/96, 4/96, 3/97, 4/97, 11/97, 3/99, 4/99

Parker, 12/89

Parris, 9/99

Parsons, 9/94

Pearce, 4/83

Perkins, 6/75, 6/76

Perring, 9/97, 8/98

Petit, 9/75

Pettit, in 1894 football team photograph

Petrel, fork-tailed, 11/77

Pickett, 9/76, 6/82, 9/86, 3/87, 3/88, 7/90, 11/91, 1/99, 11/99 (including photograph) and in 1893 cricket team photograph

Pigeon shooting match, 11/86, 4/95

Piltdown, 12/79, 1/83, 5/97

Pinnacle Pit, 1/82

Plain Park, 1/82

Plashett, The Old Ship, 2/80

Pocock, 8/94

Point, The, 7/75, 4/79, 2/80, 7/80, 6/82, 12/82, 11/90, 4/92, 11/92, 11/97, 1/98

Pollard, 2/87

Ponting, 6/86

Poor rate, 11/79, 12/98

Population (Newick), 2/77, 4/91

Postal Service / post boxes / letter boxes, 5/87, 6/93, 9/97, 6/99, 11/99

Post Office, 11/90, 9/94

Potter, 3/84, 6/84, 5/85 (including photograph), 7/88, 9/93

Powell, 5/75, 9/75, 7/76, 10/76, 10/79, 5/81, 1/84, 1/85, 2/85, 3/85, 4/85, 9/85, 10/85, 3/86, 8/86, 9/86, 10/86, 11/86, 2/87, 3/87, 8/87, 10/87, 11/87, 3/88, 5/88, 1/89, 12/89, 3/90, 11/90, 3/91, 5/91, 12/91, 4/92, 6/92, 10/92, 12/92, 1/93, 3/93, 4/93, 10/93, 6/94, 12/94, 1/95, 2/95, 4/95, 8/95, 2/96, 4/96, 8/96, 12/96, 2/97, 4/97, 11/97, 7/98, 9/98, 2/99, 7/99, 8/99, 9/99, 10/99 and in 1893 cricket team photograph and 1894 football team photograph

Pratt, 11/77

Price, 12/96

Priestly, 2/96

Primrose Day, 4/86

Primrose League (including South Saxon Habitation and Weald of Sussex Habitation), 3/86, 7/86, 8/86, 9/88, 2/89, 2/97

Prince, 5/92

Prince of Wales, 5/96

Provey, 7/75

Pump (on The Green), 6/87, 4/97, 5/97, 7/98

Pumphrey, 6/90

Quirke, 2/87

Quoits, 5/97, 5/98, 6/98

Railway (Hellingly to Sheffield Bridge), 10/79

Railway (Lewes to East Grinstead)

Planning of, 10/76, 11/76, 8/77, 3/78, 4/78, 11/78, 1/79, 2/79,

Building of (navvies, contractor etc), 2/79, 9/79, 10/79, 11/79, 12/79, 4/80, 6/80, 7/80, 8/80, 9/80, 10/80, 11/80, 12/80, 1/81, 4/81, 5/81, 6/81, 11/81, 1/82, 3/82, 7/82

Opening of, 8/82 (including photograph)

Station and stationmasters (Newick and Chailey), 1/82, 7/82, 10/82, 1/83, 10/83, 11/84, 4/86, 5/87, 1/88, 2/88, 3/88, 1/89, 7/90, 7/91, 9/91, 12/91, 7/93, 11/93, 6/94, 7/94, 7/95, 8/95, 3/97, 9/97, 5/99

Railway Reading Room, 12/79, 2/80, 9/80, 10/80, 11/80

Timetable / Special trains, 6/87, 5/91, 5/98, 10/98, 11/98, 12/98, 3/99, 5/99, 6/99, 7/99, 9/99, 11/99

Railway (Uckfield to Balcombe), 5/75

Ravenhill, 5/94, 4/97, 11/97, 3/98, 1/99, 3/99

Read, 10/95

Reading Room, 11/80, 3/91, 4/91, 3/92, 4/92, 5/92, 7/92, 10/92, 1/93, 2/93, 3/93, 5/93, 6/93, 9/93, 10/93, 12/93, 1/94, 2/94, 3/94, 4/94, 10/94, 11/94, 1/95, 2/95, 4/95, 9/95, 10/95, 11/95, 12/95, 1/96, 2/96, 3/96, 4/96, 10/96, 2/97, 5/97, 10/97, 12/97, 1/98, 2/98, 4/98, 11/98, 12/98, 1/99, 4/99, 10/99, 11/99

Rectory, 4/85, 9/85, 10/85, 1/86, 10/86, 2/87, 3/87, 1/88, 2/88, 6/88, 11/88, 1/89, 10/89, 12/89, 2/90, 9/90, 10/90, 11/90, 12/90, 1/91, 2/91, 3/91, 4/92, 5/92, 7/92, 1/93, 9/94, 11/94, 4/95, 8/95, 1/96, 4/96, 7/96, 2/97, 2/98, 2/99, 4/99, 8/99

Reed, 4/94, 5/99

Reedens, 11/77, 11/84, 11/86, 11/88, 11/89, 11/92, 10/93, 9/94, 11/97

Reilly, 12/89

Rent / Tithe Audit, 11/79, 11/87, 11/88, 11/89, 11/90, 11/97, 11/99

Rest, The, 11/97

Retreat, The, 3/93

Rhodes, 11/90

Richards, 10/88, 11/90, 8/99, 9/99

Ricketts Farm, 6/85

Ridley, 11/90, 9/99

Ringmer, 3/91

Roden, Dowager Lady, 8/92

Rogers, 5/85 (including photograph), 8/86, 1/88, 11/97, 6/99 (and in 1893 cricket team photo)

Rose Cottage, 3/90

Roser, 7/75, 11/90

Roswell, 6/75

Rotherfield Farm, 2/75, 3/78

Rotherfield Wood, 2/77, 2/78, 3/79, 7/91, 7/94

Rough, The, 11/84, 11/86, 11/90, 11/92, 4/93, 9/94, 11/94, 2/95, 9/95, 2/97

Royal Academy, 5/96

Royal Oak public house / beer house, 4/76, 11/76, 12/76, 11/78, 11/80, 5/82, 7/93, 4/95, 12/95, 11/96, 12/96, 5/97, 11/97, 11/98, 11/99, 12/99

Ruck-Keene, 12/90, 8/92

Rural Deanery of Pevensey, 6/88, 7/93, 8/96

Sadler, 12/82, 5/83, 4/84, 6/84

Salvage, 12/85, 2/97, 10/99

Saxby and Farmer, 7/82

Scarlet fever, 1/76, 9/77, 12/77, 1/78, 9/79, 10/83, 6/87, 1/88, 9/89

School

Board, 3/75, 6/75, 10/75, 1/83, 5/83, 5/84, 3/90, 3/93, 11/99

Infants, 4/81, 10/82, 11/82, 12/82, 1/83, 4/83, 5/83, 8/83, 10/83, 5/84, 8/84, 10/86, 8/87, 1/88, 8/88, 1/90, 8/92, 11/93, 3/94, 8/94, 3/97

Lady Vernon, 10/78, 7/79, 10/82, 10/83, 1/84, 5/84, 8/84, 10/85, 3/86, 10/86, 3/87, 8/87, 1/88, 8/88, 8/89, 9/89, 1/90, 8/92, 8/93, 8/94, 12/96

National Boys, 9/75, 10/75, 1/76, 3/76, 9/76, 2/77, 4/77, 12/77, 1/78, 2/78, 4/78, 8/78, 10/78, 3/79, 4/79, 5/79, 7/79, 10/79, 11/79, 2/80, 3/80, 6/80, 4/81, 5/81, 6/81, 7/81, 8/81, 10/81, 2/82, 8/82, 9/82, 11/82, 1/83, 8/83, 9/83, 2/84, 5/84, 8/84, 10/84, 12/84, 1/85, 2/85, 6/85, 9/85, 10/85, 11/85, 12/85, 1/86, 2/86, 3/86, 4/86, 5/86, 8/86, 10/86, 1/87, 4/87, 5/87, 6/87, 8/87, 10/87, 11/87, 1/88, 2/88, 5/88, 8/88, 9/88, 11/88, 1/89, 2/89, 3/89, 5/89, 8/89, 9/89, 10/89, 11/89, 12/89, 1/90, 2/90, 4/90, 5/90, 6/90, 12/90, 2/91, 3/91, 4/91, 5/91, 8/91, 9/91, 12/91, 1/92, 3/92, 4/92, 8/92, 12/92, 4/93, 6/93, 9/93, 12/93, 3/94, 4/94, 5/94, 9/94, 11/94, 12/94, 1/95, 3/95, 4/95, 8/95, 9/95, 11/95, 12/95, 1/96, 2/96, 3/96, 4/96, 5/96, 9/96, 11/96, 12/96, 2/97, 4/97, 5/97, 9/97, 10/97, 11/97, 12/97, 1/98, 2/98, 12/98, 3/99, 6/99, 9/99, 10/99, 11/99, 12/99

Sunday, 8/80, 10/80, 7/83, 12/85, 1/87, 1/88, 1/89, 1/90, 12/90, 12/91, 9/92, 12/92, 12/93, 12/94, 12/95, 12/97, 10/98

Schoolhouse Farm, 11/90

Sclater, 2/75, 6/75, 9/75, 10/76, 7/77, 9/77, 1/78, 11/79, 5/80, 3/81, 6/82 (including photograph), 1/83, 8/83, 10/83, 6/84, 8/84, 10/84, 6/85, 8/85, 10/85, 5/86, 7/86, 10/86, 3/87, 7/87, 9/87, 2/88, 5/88, 3/89, 11/89, 3/90, 10/90, 11/90, 3/91, 4/92, 8/92, 10/92, 1/93, 3/93, 8/93, 9/93, 10/94, 10/95, 11/97 (including photograph), 12/97, 1/98, 2/98, 5/98, 8/98, 12/98, 6/99, 8/99

Scott, 5/86, 5/89, 3/98, 3/99

Searles, 12/79

Selby, 12/89, 5/90

Sheffield Arms, 9/78, 7/95

Sheffield, Lord / Earl, 10/76, 11/76, 3/77, 7/77, 3/82, 7/83, 5/84, 7/84,
    5/85, 5/86, 12/86, 3/87, 10/87, 11/88, 12/88, 4/89, 5/90, 5/91,
    7/91, 8/91, 11/91, 5/92, 6/92, 4/93, 5/93, 5/94, 7/94, 2/95,
    7/95, 5/96

Sheffield Park, 8/79, 7/83, 5/84, 7/84, 5/85, 5/86, 3/87, 10/87, 7/89,
    5/90, 7/90, 1/91, 5/91, 7/91, 7/92, 9/92, 5/93, 5/94, 7/94, 2/95,
    7/95, 5/96

Sheffield Park Station, 6/86, 4/90, 7/91, 7/94, 7/95, 5/96

Shenstone, 1/80

Sheppard, 8/80

Shiffner, 9/76, 2/92, 8/92, 12/92

Shoemakers shop, 7/89

Sidesmen, 3/91, 4/97

Simmons, 9/98, 9/99

Skating, 1/91, 1/93, 2/95

Slender, 5/96

Slugs, 5/89

Smith, 8/76, 4/77, 12/77, 4/79, 9/86, 11/90, 9/94, 10/94, 12/94, 10/95,
    9/98, 6/99, 9/99, 12/99

Smithers, 10/92

Snells Field, 9/75

Society for the Propagation of the Gospel, 11/86, 4/87, 3/91, 2/97

Society for Protection of Ancient Buildings, 3/86

South Africans, cricket team, 5/94

Southdown Foxhounds, 10/78, 12/79, 1/80, 12/83, 2/94, 2/97

South Saxon Lodge of Oddfellows, 10/93

Spratt, 4/95

Spring, 7/98

Standen, 5/87, 7/87, 10/87, 11/87

Staplehurst, 11/76, 11/78, 8/80, 11/80, 10/87, 4/95, 9/99

Starr, 5/88, 7/88

Stead, 7/78

Stephens, 11/80, 9/81, 9/91

Stevens, 9/98, 12/98

Stevenson, 7/99

Stoolball, 8/79, 8/89, 8/96, 6/99

Strawberries, 8/91

Strawberry Gardens, 10/99

Streater, in 1894 football team photograph

String Band (Newick), 2/76, 3/91

Sturt, 1/84, 4/85

Sumner-Smith, 10/78

Surveyor of Highways, 3/86, 3/87, 4/89, 3/91, 3/93

Sussex County Cricket Club, 3/81

Sutton Hall, 6/85

Swaysland and Swaysland Academy, 9/80, 10/80, 2/81

Tanyard, 10/99

Tatton, 10/78

Taylor, 5/87

Teachers Orphanage and Orphan Fund and Benevolent and Orphan
Fund, 3/79, 5/96

Telegraph, 7/95

Thomas, 9/85

Thompson, 4/80, 11/94

Tidy, 3/84, 6/84, 5/85 (including photograph), 10/85, 3/88, 7/90
(including photograph), 3/92, 5/92, 10/92, 1/93, 12/94, 4/95,
10/97, 1/98, 9/98, 11/99 (including photograph)

Tilehouse Farm, 10/83, 11/90

Tingley, 9/94

Tithe Audit – see Rent Audit

Towner, 7/89

Tradesman Club, 1/75

Turner, 11/80, 11/81, 12/89, 11/90, 7/91, 12/91, 4/93, 8/94, 6/97, 9/99

Turnpike, 1/79

Uckfield

    Brass Band, 5/92

    Chess, 2/93, 12/93, 2/94, 1/95

    Fire Brigade, 7/95, 12/96

    Railway Line, 5/75

Uridge, 1/80, 10/82
Varnham, 8/94
Veness, 3/95
Vernon, Lady (school) – see School
Verrall, 9/75
Vestry meeting – see Parish meeting
Victoria, Queen – see Jubilee
Vinall, 3/82
Vuggles, 9/77, 11/90
Waghorn, 3/77
Wakeford, 11/90, 12/90
Walford, 1/83, 12/85
Walls, 5/85 (including photograph)
Wallis, 5/93, 2/94
Wapsbourne Farm, 2/78
Wapsbourne Wood, 2/78
Warner, 8/87, 8/89, 9/89
Warnett, in 1894 football team photograph
Warren, The, 2/80
Waters, 4/84, 5/84, 6/84
Watson, 4/75, 2/78, 3/78 (including photograph), 8/82, 6/86, 11/90, 12/98, 11/99 (including photograph)
Watts, 9/91, 11/93, 9/98, 9/99 (and in 1894 football team photograph)
Weald of Sussex Habitation – see Primrose League
Wells, 12/92
Western Road, 12/92, 6/94, 9/94, 11/94, 10/99
Weston, 6/75, 7/75, 8/76, 2/77, 7/77, 1/82, 1/86, 9/86, 11/88, 9/93, 6/99, 9/99, 11/99 (including photograph)
Wet Wood, 3/79
Wheatland, 11/80, 9/86, 9/94, 9/99 (and in 1894 football team photograph)
Wheelwright, 7/80, 3/98
Whist, 11/89, 1/91, 3/92, 3/93, 9/93, 5/94, 1/95, 4/95, 10/95, 11/95, 12/95, 1/96, 2/96, 3/96, 1/97, 2/97, 11/97, 12/99, 2/99, 3/99
Whitfield, 1/95
Whitting, 10/97

Whooping cough, 9/88
Wicks, 4/85
Williams, 12/86, 12/94, 9/98
Wimpress, 4/92, 10/94
Wivesfield, 5/94
Women's Jubilee Offering Fund, 4/87
Wood, 5/78, 1/84, 3/84, 6/84, 9/86, 2/87, 10/87, 2/88, 1/90, 10/92, 4/93, 5/94, 12/94, 4/95, 7/95, 3/98, 7/98, 8/98, 9/98, 3/99, 6/99, 7/99, 9/99 (and in 1893 cricket team photograph and 1894 football team photograph)
Woodbine Farm, 9/97, 5/99
Woodriffe, 2/97
Workhouse field, 4/95, 5/95, 3/96
Yew Villa, 6/82, 7/89
Yollond, 7/82, 10/82
York, Duke of, 6/93, 7/93, 10/93
Young, 1/76, 4/77, 8/77
Zion Chapel, 6/76, 6/77, 6/82, 6/84, 9/85, 2/86, 6/86, 6/91, 6/94, 6/95, 9/95, 10/99